Correspondence of Benedict de Spinoza

Correspondence of Benedict de Spinoza

by Benedict de Spinoza
Translated from the Latin by R. H. M. Elwes

Table of Contents

LETTER I.
HENRY OLDENBURG 2 TO B. DE SPINOZA.

[Oldenburg, after complimenting Spinoza, asks him to enter into a philosophical correspondence.]

ILLUSTRIOUS Sir, and most worthy friend,—SO painful to me was the separation from you the other day after our meeting in your retreat at Rhijnsburg, that it is my first endeavour, now that I am returned to England, to renew, as far as is possible by correspondence, my intercourse with you. Solid learning, conjoined with courtesy and refinement of manners (wherewith both nature and art have most amply endowed you), carries with it such charms as to command the love of every honourable and liberally-educated man. Let us then, most excellent sir, join hands in sincere friendship, and let us foster the feeling with every zealous endeavour and kind office in our power. Whatever my poor means can furnish I beg you to look on as your own. Allow me in return to claim a share in the riches of your talents, as I may do without inflicting any loss on yourself.

We conversed at Rhijnsburg of God, of extension, of infinite thought, of the differences and agreements between these, of the nature of the connection between the human soul and body, and further, of the principles of the Cartesian and Baconian philosophies.

But, as we then spoke of these great questions merely cursorily and by the way, and as my mind has been not a little tormented with them since, I will appeal to the rights of our newly cemented friendship, and most affectionately beg you to give me at somewhat greater length your opinion on the subjects I have mentioned. On two points especially I ask for enlightenment, if I may presume so far; first: In what do you place the true distinction between thought and matter? secondly: What do you consider to be the chief defects in the Cartesian and Baconian philosophies, and how do you think they might best be removed, and something more sound substituted? The more freely you write to me on these and similar subjects, the more closely will you tie the bonds of our friendship, and the stricter will be the obligation laid on me to repay you, as far as possible, with similar services.

There is at present in the press a collection of physiological discourses written by an Englishman of noble family and distinguished learning. 1 They treat of the nature and elasticity of the air, as proved by forty-three experiments; also of its fluidity, solidity, and other analogous matters. As soon as the work is published, I shall make a point of sending it to you by any friend who may be crossing the sea. Meanwhile, farewell, and remember your friend, who is

Yours, in all affection and zeal,
HENRY OLDENBURG.
London, 12/26 Aug., 1661.

LETTER II.
SPINOZA TO OLDENBURG.

[Answer to Letter I. Spinoza defines "God," and "attribute," and sends definitions, axioms, and first four propositions of Book I. of Ethics. Some errors of Bacon and Descartes discussed.]

Illustrious Sir,—How pleasant your friendship is to me, you may yourself judge, if your modesty will allow you to reflect on the abundance of your own excellences. Indeed the thought of these makes me seem not a little bold in entering into such a compact, the more so when I consider that between friends all things, and especially things spiritual, ought to be in common. However, this must lie at the charge of your modesty and kindness rather than of myself. You have been willing to lower yourself through the former and to fill me with the abundance of the latter, till I am no longer afraid to accept the close friendship, which you hold out to me, and which you deign to ask of me in return; no effort on my part shall be spared to render it lasting.

As for my mental endowments, such as they are, I would willingly allow you to share them, even though I knew it would be to my own great hindrance. But this is not meant as an excuse for denying to you what you ask by the rights of friendship. I will therefore endeavour to explain my opinions on the topics you touched on; though I scarcely hope, unless your kindness intervene, that 1 shall thus draw the bonds of our friendship closer.

I will then begin by speaking briefly of God, Whom I define as a Being consisting in infinite attributes, whereof each is infinite or supremely perfect after its kind. You must observe that by attribute I mean eves y thing,

which is conceived through itself and in itself, so that the conception of it does not involve the conception of anything else. For instance, extension is conceived through itself and in itself, but motion is not. The latter is conceived through something else, for the conception of it implies extension.

That the definition above given of God is true appears from the fact, that by God we mean a Being supremely perfect and absolutely infinite. That such a Being exists may easily be proved from the definition; but as this is not the place for such proof, I will pass it over. What I am bound here to prove, in order to satisfy the first inquiry of my distinguished questioner, are the following consequences; first, that in the universe there cannot exist two substances without their differing utterly in essence; secondly, that substance cannot be produced or created—existence pertains to its actual essence; thirdly, that all substance must be infinite or supremely perfect after its kind.

When these points have been demonstrated, my distinguished questioner will readily perceive my drift, if he reflects at the same time on the definition of God. In order to prove them clearly and briefly, I can think of nothing better than to submit them to the bar of your judgment proved in the geometrical method. 1 I therefore enclose them separately and await your verdict upon them.

Again, you ask me what errors I detect in the Cartesian and Baconian philosophies. It is not my custom to expose the errors of others, nevertheless I will yield to your request. The first and the greatest error is, that these philosophers have strayed so far from the knowledge of the first cause and origin of all things; the second is, that they did not know the true nature of the human mind; the third, that they never grasped the true cause of error. The necessity for correct knowledge on these three points can only be ignored by persons completely devoid of learning and training.

That they have wandered astray from the knowledge of the first cause, and of the human mind, may easily be gathered from the truth of the three propositions given above; I therefore devote myself entirely to the demonstration of the third error. Of Bacon I shall say very little, for he speaks very confusedly on the point, and works out scarcely any proofs: he simply narrates. In the first place he assumes, that the human intellect is liable to err, not only through the fallibility of the senses, but also solely through its own nature, and that it frames its conceptions in accordance with the analogy of its own nature, not with the analogy of the universe, so that it is like a mirror receiving rays from external objects unequally, and mingling its own nature with the nature of things, &c.

Secondly, that the human intellect is, by reason of its own nature, prone to abstractions; such things as are in flux it feigns to be constant, &c.

Thirdly, that the human intellect continually augments, and is unable to come to a stand or to rest content. The other causes which he assigns may all be reduced to the one Cartesian principle, that the human will is free and more extensive than the intellect, or, as Verulam himself more confusedly puts it, that "the understanding is not a dry light, but receives infusion from the will." 1 (We may here observe that Verulam often employs "intellect" as synonymous with mind, differing in this respect from Descartes). This cause, then, leaving aside the others as unimportant, I shall show to be false; indeed its falsity would be evident to its supporters, if they would consider, that will in general differs from this or that particular volition in the same way as whiteness differs from this or that white object, or humanity from this or that man. It is, therefore, as impossible to conceive, that will is the cause of a given volition, as to conceive that humanity is the cause of Peter and Paul.

Hence, as will is merely an entity of the reason, and cannot be called the cause of particular volitions, and as some cause is needed for the existence of such volitions, these latter cannot be called free, but are necessarily such as they are determined by their causes; lastly, according to Descartes, errors are themselves particular volitions; hence it necessarily follows that errors, or, in other words, particular volitions, are not free, but are determined by external causes, and in nowise by the will. This is what I undertook to prove.

LETTER III.
OLDENBURG TO SPINOZA.

[Oldenburg propounds several questions concerning God and His existence, thought, and the axioms of Eth. I. He also informs Spinoza of a philosophical society, and promises to send Boyle's book.]

Most Excellent Friend, Your learned letter has been delivered to me, and read with great pleasure.

I highly approve of your geometrical method of proof, but I must set it down to my dulness, that I cannot follow with readiness what you set forth with such accuracy. Suffer me, then, I beg, to expose the slowness of my understanding, while I put the following questions, and beg of you to answer them.

First. Do you clearly and indisputably understand solely from the definition you have given of God, that such a Being exists? For my part, when I reflect that definitions contain only the conceptions formed by our minds, and that our mind forms many conceptions of things which do not exist, and is very fertile in multiplying and amplifying what it has conceived, I do not yet see, that from the conception I have of God I can infer God's existence. I am able by a mental combination of all the perfections I perceive in men, in animals, in vegetables, in minerals, &c., to conceive and to form an idea of some single substance uniting in itself all such excellences; indeed my mind is able to multiply and augment such excellences indefinitely; it may thus figure forth for itself a most perfect and excellent Being, but there would be no reason thence to conclude that such a Being actually exists.

Secondly. I wish to ask, whether you think it unquestionable, that body cannot be limited by thought, or thought by body; seeing that it still remains undecided, what thought is, whether it be a physical motion or a spiritual act quite distinct from body?

Thirdly. Do you reckon the axioms, which you have sent to me, as indemonstrable principles known by the light of nature and needing no proof? Perhaps the first is of this nature, but I do not see how the other three can be placed in a like category. The second assumes that nothing exists in the universe save substances and accidents, but many persons would say that time and place cannot be classed either as one or the other. Your third axiom, that things having different attributes have no quality in common, is so far from being clear to me, that its contrary seems to be shown in the whole universe. All things known to us agree in certain respects and differ in others. Lastly, your fourth axiom, that when things have no quality in common, one cannot be produced by another, is not so plain to my groping intelligence as to stand in need of no further illumination. God has nothing actually in common with created things, yet nearly all of us believe Him to be their cause.

As you see that in my opinion your axioms are not established beyond all the assaults of doubt, you will readily gather that the propositions you have based upon them do not appear to me absolutely firm. The more I reflect upon them, the more are doubts suggested to my mind concerning them.

As to the first, I submit that two men are two substances with the same attribute, inasmuch as both are rational; whence I infer that there can be two substances with the same attribute.

As to the second, I opine that, as nothing can be its own cause, it is hardly within the scope of our intellect to pronounce on the truth of the proposition, that substance cannot be produced even by any other substance. Such a proposition asserts all substances to be self-caused, and all and each to be independent of one another, thus making so many gods, and therefore denying the first cause of all things. This, I willingly confess, I cannot understand, unless you will be kind enough to explain your theory on this sublime subject somewhat more fully and simply, informing me what may be the origin and mode of production of substances, and the mutual interdependence and subordination of things. I most strenuously beg and conjure you by that friendship which we have entered into, to answer me freely and faithfully on these points; you may rest assured, that everything which you think fit to communicate to me will remain untampered with and safe, for I will never allow anything to become public through me to your hurt or disadvantage. In our philosophical society we proceed diligently as far as opportunity offers with our experiments and observations, lingering over the compilation of the history of mechanic arts, with the idea that the forms and qualities of things can best be explained from mechanical principles, and that all natural effects can be produced through motion, shape, and consistency, without reference to inexplicable forms or occult qualities, which are but the refuge of ignorance.

I will send the book I promised, whenever the Dutch Ambassadors send (as they frequently do) a messenger to the Hague, or whenever some other friend whom I can trust goes your way. I beg you to excuse my prolixity and freedom, and simply ask you to take in good part, as one friend from another, the straightforward and unpolished reply I have sent to your letter, believing me to be without deceit or affectation,

Yours most faithfully,
HENRY OLDENBURG.
London, 27 Sept., 1661.

LETTER IV.
SPINOZA TO OLDENBURG.

[Spinoza answers some of Oldenburg's questions and doubts, but has not time to reply to all, as he is just setting out for Amsterdam.]

Illustrious Sir,—As I was starting for Amsterdam, where I intend staying for a week or two, I received your most welcome letter, and noted the objections you raise to the three propositions I sent you. Not having time to reply fully, I will confine myself to these three.

To the first I answer, that not from every definition does the existence of the thing defined follow, but only (as I showed in a note appended to the three propositions) from the definition or idea of an attribute, that is (as I explained fully in the definition given of God) of a thing conceived through and in itself. The reason for this distinction was pointed out, if I mistake not, in the above-mentioned note sufficiently clearly at any rate for a philosopher, who is assumed to be aware of the difference between a fiction and a clear and distinct idea, and also of the truth of the axiom that every definition or clear and distinct idea is true. When this has been duly noted, I do not see what more is required for the solution of your first question.

I therefore proceed to the solution of the second, wherein you seem to admit that, if thought does not belong to the nature of extension, then extension will not be limited by thought; your doubt only involves the example given. But observe, I beg, if we say that extension is not limited by extension but by thought, is not this the same as saying that extension is not infinite absolutely, but only as far as extension is concerned, in other words, infinite after its kind? But you say: perhaps thought is a corporeal action be it so, though I by no means grant it: you, at any rate, will not deny that extension, in so far as it is extension, is not thought, and this is all that is required for explaining my definition and proving the third proposition.

Thirdly. You proceed to object, that my axioms ought not to be ranked as universal notions. I will not dispute this point with you; but you further hesitate as to their truth, seeming to desire to show that their contrary is more probable. Consider, I beg, the definition which I gave of substance and attribute, for on that they all depend.. When I say that I mean by substance that which is conceived through and in itself; and that I mean by modification or accident that, which is in something else, and is conceived through that wherein it is, evidently it follows that substance is by nature prior to its accidents. For without the former the latter can neither be nor be conceived. Secondly, it follows that, besides substances and accidents, nothing exists really or externally to the intellect. For everything is conceived either through itself or through something else, and the conception of it either involves or does not involve the conception of something else. Thirdly, it follows that things which possess different attributes have nothing in common. For by attribute I have explained that I mean something, of which the conception does not involve the conception of anything else. Fourthly and lastly, it follows that, if two things have nothing in common, one cannot be the cause of the other. For, as there would be nothing in common between the effect and the cause, the whole effect would spring from nothing. As for your contention that God has nothing actually in common with created things, I have maintained the exact opposite in my definition. I said that God is a Being consisting of infinite attributes, whereof each one is infinite or supremely perfect after its kind. With regard to what you say concerning my first proposition, I beg you, my friend, to bear in mind, that men are not created but born, and that their bodies already exist before birth, though under different forms. You draw the conclusion, wherein I fully concur, that, if one particle of matter be annihilated, the whole of extension would forthwith vanish. My second proposition does not make many gods but only one, to wit, a Being consisting of infinite attributes, &c.

LETTER V.
OLDENBURG TO SPINOZA.

[Oldenburg sends Boyle's book, and laments that Spinoza has not been able to answer all his doubts.]

Most respected Friend, Please accept herewith the book I promised you, and write me in answer your opinion on it, especially on the remarks about nitre, and about fluidity, and solidity. I owe you the warmest thanks for your learned second letter, which I received to-day, but I greatly grieve that your journey to Amsterdam prevented you from answering all my doubts. I beg you will supply the omission, as soon as you have leisure. You have much enlightened me in your last letter, but have not yet dispelled all my darkness; this result will, I believe, be happily accomplished, when you send me clear and distinct information concerning the first origin of things. Hitherto I have been somewhat in doubt as to the cause from which, and the manner in which things took their origin, also, as to what is the nature of their connection with the first cause, if such there be. All that I hear or read on the subject seems inconclusive. Do you then, my very learned master, act, as it were, as my torch-bearer in the matter. You will have no reason to doubt my confidence and gratitude. Such is the earnest petition of

Yours most faithfully,
HENRY OLDENBURG.

LETTER VI.
SPINOZA TO OLDENBURG.

[Containing detailed criticisms by Spinoza of Robert Boyle's book.]
Omitted.

LETTER VII.
OLDENBURG TO SPINOZA.

[After thanking Spinoza, in the name of himself and Boyle, Oldenburg mentions the foundation of the Royal Society, and begs his correspondent to publish his theological and philosophical works.]

The body of philosophers which I formerly mentioned to you has now, by the king's grace, been constituted as a Royal Society, and furnished with a public charter, whereby distinguished privileges are conferred upon it, and an excellent prospect afforded of endowing it with the necessary revenues.

I would by all means advise you not to begrudge to the learned those works in philosophy and theology, which you have composed with the talent that distinguishes you. Publish them, I beg, whatever be the verdict of petty theologians. Your country is free; the course of philosophy should there be free also. Your own prudence will, doubtless, suggest to you, that your ideas and opinions should be put forth as quietly as possible. For the rest, commit the issue to fortune. Come, then, good sir, cast away all fear of exciting against you the pigmies of our time. Long enough have we sacrificed to ignorance and pedantry. Let us spread the sails of true knowledge, and explore the recesses of nature more thoroughly than hereto fore. Your meditations can, I take it, be printed in your country with impunity; nor need any scandal among the learned be dreaded because of them. If these be your patrons and supporters (and I warrant me you will find them so), why should you dread the carpings of ignorance? I will not let you go, my honoured friend, till I have gained my request; nor will I ever, so far as in me lies, allow thoughts of such importance as yours to rest in eternal silence. I earnestly beg you to communicate to me, as soon as you conveniently can, your decision in the matter. Perhaps events will occur here not unworthy of your knowledge. The Society I have mentioned will now proceed more strenuously on its course, and, if peace continues on our shores, will possibly illustrate the republic of letters with some extraordinary achievement. Farewell, excellent sir, and believe me,

Your most zealous and friendly,
HENRY OLDENBURG.

LETTER VIII.
OLDENBURG TO SPINOZA.

[After further replying to Spinoza's criticisms on Boyle's book, Oldenburg again exhorts his correspondent to publish.]

I now proceed to the question which has arisen between us. First, permit me to ask you whether you have finished the important little work, in which you treat "of the origin of things and their dependence on the first cause, and of the improvement of our understanding." Truly, my dear sir, I believe nothing more pleasing or acceptable to men of true learning and discrimination could possibly be published than such a treatise. This is what a man of your talent and disposition should look to, far more than the gratification of theologians of our time and fashion. The latter have less regard for truth than for their own convenience. I, therefore, conjure you, by the bond of our friendship, by every duty of increasing and proclaiming the truth, not to begrudge us, or withhold from us your writings o these subjects. If anything of greater importance than I can foresee prevents you from publishing the work, I earnestly charge you to give me a summary of it by letter.

Another book is soon to be published by the learned Boyle, which I will send you as an exchange. I will add papers, which will acquaint you with the whole constitution of our Royal Society, whereof I, with twenty others, am on the Council, and, with one other, am Secretary. I have no time to discourse of any further subjects. All the confidence which honest intentions can inspire, all the readiness to serve, which the smallness of my powers will permit, I pledge to you, and am heartily,

Dear sir, yours wholly,

H. OLDENBURG.

London, 3 April, 1663.

LETTER IX.
SPINOZA TO OLDENBURG.

[Spinoza informs Oldenburg that he has removed to Rhijnsburg, and has spent some time at Amsterdam for the purpose of publishing the "Principles of Cartesian Philosophy." He then replies to Boyle's objections.]

DISTINGUISHED SIR,—I have at length received your long wished for letter, and am at liberty to answer it. But, before I do so, I will briefly tell you, what has prevented my replying before. When I removed my household goods here in April, I set out for Amsterdam. While there certain friends asked me to impart to them a treatise containing, in brief, the second part of the principles of Descartes treated geometrically, together with some of the chief points treated of in metaphysics, which I had formerly dictated to a youth, to whom I did not wish to teach my own opinions openly. They further requested me, at the first opportunity, to compose a similar treatise on the first part. Wishing to oblige my friends, I at once set myself to the task, which I finished in a fortnight, and handed over to them. They then asked for leave to print it, which I readily granted on the condition that one of them should, under my supervision, clothe it in more elegant phraseology, and add a little preface warning readers that I do not acknowledge all the opinions there set forth as my own, inasmuch as I hold the exact contrary to much that is there written, illustrating the fact by one or two examples. All this the friend who took charge of the treatise promised to do, and this is the cause for my prolonged stay in Amsterdam. Since I returned to this village, I have hardly been able to call my time my own, because of the friends who have been kind enough to visit me. At last, my dear friend, a moment has come, when I can relate these occurrences to you, and inform you why I allow this treatise to see the light. It may be that on this occasion some of those, who hold the foremost positions in my country, will be found desirous of seeing the rest of my writings, which I acknowledge as my own; they will thus take care that I am enabled to publish them without any danger of infringing the laws of the land. If this be as I think, I shall doubtless publish at once; if things fall out otherwise, I would rather be silent than obtrude my opinions on men, in defiance of my country, and thus render them hostile to me. I therefore hope, my friend, that you will not chafe at having to wait a short time longer; you shall then receive from me either the treatise printed, or the summary of it which you ask for. If meanwhile you would like to have one or two copies of the work now in the press,

I will satisfy your wish, as soon as I know of it and of means to send the book conveniently.

[The rest of the letter is taken up with criticisms on Boyle's book.]

LETTERS X.-XIV. 1

[Contain further correspondence concerning Boyle's book, and kindred subjects.]

LETTER XIII.A.
OLDENBURG TO SPINOZA.

[The place of this letter is between Letters XIII. and XIV. It was written apparently in September, 1665. It mentions the plague, which was then at its height, the war, and the labours of the Royal Society, and especially of Boyle. Then comes the passage here given. The letter terminates with references to the comets, and to Huyghens.]

I see that you are engaged not so much in philosophy as in theology, if I may say so. That is, you are recording your thoughts about angels, prophecy, and miracles, but you are doing this, perhaps, in a philosophical manner; however that may be, I am certain that the work 1 is worthy of you, and that I am most anxious to have it. Since these most difficult times prevent free intercourse, I beg at least that you will not disdain to signify to me in your next letter 2 your design and aim in this writing of yours.

Here we are daily expecting news of a second 3 naval battle, unless indeed your fleet has retired into port. Virtue, 4 the nature of which you hint is being discussed among your friends, belongs to wild beasts not to men. For if men acted according to the guidance of reason, they would not so tear one another in pieces, as they evidently do. But what is the good of my complaining? Vices will exist while men do; 5 but yet they are not continuous, but compensated by the interposition of better things.

LETTER XV.
SPINOZA TO OLDENBURG.

[Spinoza writes to his friend concerning the reasons which lead us to believe, that "every part of nature agrees with the whole, and is associated with all other parts." He also makes a few remarks about Huyghens.]

Distinguished Sir,—For the encouragement to pursue my speculations given me by yourself and the distinguished R. Boyle, I return you my best thanks. I proceed as far as my slender abilities will allow me, with full confidence in your aid and kindness. When you ask me my opinion on the question raised concerning our knowledge of the means, whereby each part of nature agrees with its whole, and the manner in which it is associated with the remaining parts, I presume you are asking for the reasons which induce us to believe, that each part of nature agrees with its whole, and is associated with the remaining parts. For as to the means whereby the parts are really associated, and each part agrees with its whole, I told you in my former letter that I am in ignorance. To answer such a question, we should have to know the whole of nature and its several parts. I will therefore endeavour to show the reason, which led me to make the statement; but I will premise that I do not attribute to nature either beauty or deformity, order or confusion. Only in relation to our imagination can things be called beautiful or deformed, ordered or confused.

By the association of parts, then, I merely mean that the laws or nature of one part adapt themselves to the laws or nature of another part, so as to cause the least possible inconsistency. As to the whole and the parts, I mean that a given number of things are parts of a whole, in so far as the nature of each of them is adapted to the nature of the rest, so that they all, as far as possible, agree together. On the other hand, in so far as they do not agree, each of them forms, in our mind, a separate idea, and is to that extent considered as a whole, not as a part. For instance, when the parts of lymph, chyle, &c., combine, according to the proportion of the figure and size of each, so as to evidently unite, and form one fluid, the chyle, lymph, &c., considered under this aspect, are part of the blood; but, in so far as we consider the particles of lymph as differing in figure and size from the particles of chyle, we shall consider each of the two as a whole, not as a part.

Let us imagine, with your permission, a little worm, living in the blood, able to distinguish by sight the particles of blood, lymph, &c., and to reflect on the manner in which each particle, on meeting with another particle, either is repulsed, or communicates a portion of its own motion. This little worm would live in the blood, in the same way as we live in a part of the universe, and would consider each particle of blood, not as a part, but as a whole. He would be unable to determine, how all the parts are modified by the general nature of blood, and are compelled by it to adapt themselves, so as to stand in a fixed relation to one another. For, if we imagine that there are no causes external to the blood, which could communicate fresh movements to it, nor any space beyond the blood, nor any bodies whereto the particles of blood could communicate their motion, it is certain that the blood would always remain in the same state, and its particles would undergo no modifications, save those which may be conceived as arising from the relations of motion existing between the lymph, the chyle, &c. The blood would then always have to be considered as a whole, not as a part. But, as there exist, as a matter of fact, very many causes which modify, in a given manner, the nature of the blood, and are, in turn, modified thereby, it follows that other motions and other relations arise in the blood, springing not from the mutual relations of its parts only, but from the mutual relations between the blood as a whole and external causes. Thus the blood comes to be regarded as a part, not as a whole. So much for the whole and the part.

All natural bodies can and ought to be considered in the same way as we have here considered the blood, for all bodies are surrounded by others, and are mutually determined to exist and operate in a fixed and definite proportion, while the relations between motion and rest in the sum total of them, that is, in the whole universe, remain unchanged. Hence it follows that each body, in so far as it exists as modified in a particular manner, must be considered as a part of the whole universe, as agreeing with the whole, and associated with the remaining parts. As the nature of the universe is not limited, like the nature of blood, but is absolutely infinite, its parts are by this nature of infinite power infinitely modified, and compelled to undergo infinite variations. But, in respect to substance, I conceive that each part has a more close union with its whole. For, as I said in my first letter 1 (addressed to you while I was still at Rhijnsburg), substance being infinite in its nature, 2 it follows, as I endeavoured to show, that each part belongs to the nature of substance, and, without it, can neither be nor be conceived.

You see, therefore, how and why I think that the human body is a part of nature. As regards the human mind, I believe that it also is a part of nature; for I maintain that there exists in nature an infinite power of thinking, which, in so far as it is infinite, contains subjectively the whole of nature, and its thoughts proceed in the same manner as nature—that is, in the sphere of ideas. 3 Further, I take the human mind to be identical with this said power, not in so far as it is infinite, and perceives the whole of nature, but in so far as it is finite, and perceives only the human body; in this manner, I maintain that the human mind is a part of an infinite understanding.

But to explain, and accurately prove, all these and kindred questions, would take too long; and I do not think you expect as much of me at present. I am afraid that I may have mistaken your meaning, and given an answer to a different question from that which you asked. Please inform me on this point.

You write in your last letter, that I hinted that nearly all the Cartesian laws of motion are false. What I said was, if I remember rightly, that Huyghens thinks so; I myself do not impeach any of the laws except the sixth, concerning which I think Huyghens is also in error. I asked you at the same time to communicate to me the experiment made according to that hypothesis in your

Royal Society; as you have not replied, I infer that you are not at liberty to do so. The above-mentioned Huyghens is entirely occupied in polishing lenses. He has fitted up for the purpose a handsome workshop, in which he can also construct moulds. What will be the result I know not, nor, to speak the truth, do I greatly care. Experience has sufficiently taught me, that the free hand is better and more sure than any machine for polishing spherical moulds. I can tell you nothing certain as yet about the success of the clocks or the date of Huyghens' journey to France.

LETTER XVI.
OLDENBURG TO SPINOZA.

[After some remarks on Spinoza's last letter, and an account of experiments at the Royal Society and at Oxford, Oldenburg mentions ca report about the return of the Jews to Palestine].

But I pass on to politics. Everyone here is talking of a report that the Jews, after remaining scattered for more than two thousand years, are about to return to their country. Few here believe in it, but many desire it. Please tell your friend what you hear and think on the matter. For my part, unless the news is confirmed from trustworthy sources at Constantinople, which is the place chiefly concerned, I shall not believe it. I should like to know, what the Jews of Amsterdam have heard about the matter, and how they are affected by such important tidings which, if true, would assuredly seem to harbinger the end of the world. Believe me to be

Yours most zealously,
HENRY OLDENBURG
London, 8 Dec., 1665.
P.S. I will shortly tell you the opinion of our philosophers on the recent comets.

LETTER XVII.
OLDENBURG TO SPINOZA.

[Oldenburg thanks Spinoza for the Tractatus Theoligico-Politicus despatched but not received, and modifies an adverse verdict expressed in a former letter (now lost).]

I was unwilling to let pass the convenient opportunity offered me by the journey to Holland of the learned Dr. Bourgeois, an adherent of the Reformed religion, for expressing my thanks a few weeks ago for your treatise forwarded to me, but not yet arrived. But I am doubtful whether my letter was duly delivered. I indicated in them my opinion on the treatise; but on deeper and more careful inspection I now think that my verdict was hasty. Certain arguments seemed to me to be urged at the expense of religion, as measured by the standard supplied by the common run of theologians and the received formulas of creeds which are evidently biassed. But a closer consideration of the whole subject convinced me, that you are far from attempting any injury to true religion and sound philosophy, but, on the contrary, strive to exalt and establish the true object of the Christian religion and the divine loftiness of fruitful philosophy.

Now that I believe that this is your fixed purpose, I would most earnestly beg you to have the kindness to write frequently and explain the nature of what you are now preparing and considering with this object to your old and sincere friend, who is all eager for the happy issue of so lofty a design. I sacredly promise you, that I will not divulge a syllable to anyone, if you enjoin silence; I will only endeavour gently to prepare the minds of good and wise men for the reception of those truths, which you will some day bring before a wider public, and I will try to dispel the prejudices, which have been conceived against your doctrines. Unless I am quite mistaken, you have an insight deeper than common into the nature and powers of the human mind, and its union with the human body. I earnestly beg you to favour me with your reflections on this subject. Farewell, most excellent Sir, and favour the devoted admirer of your teaching and virtue,

HENRY OLDENBURG.

London, 8 June, 1675. 1

LETTER XVIII.
OLDENBURG TO SPINOZA.

[Oldenburg rejoices at the renewal of correspondence, and alludes to the five books of the Ethics which Spinoza (in a letter now lost) had announced his intention of publishing.]

Our correspondence being thus happily renewed, I should be unwilling to fall short of a friend's duty in the exchange of letters. I understand from your answer delivered to me on July 5, that you intend to publish your treatise in five parts. Allow me, I beg, to warn you by the sincerity of your affection for me, not to insert any passages which may seem to discourage the practice of religion and virtue; especially as nothing is more sought after in this degenerate and evil age than doctrines of the kind, which seem to give countenance to rampant vice.

However, I will not object to receiving a few copies of the said treatise. I will only ask you that, when the time arrives, they may be entrusted to a Dutch merchant living in London, who will see that they are forwarded to me. There is no need to mention, that books of the kind in question have been sent to me: if they arrive safely to my keeping, I do not doubt that I can conveniently dispose of some copies to my friends here and there, and can obtain a just price for them. Farewell, and when you have leisure write to

Yours most zealously,
HENRY OLDENBURG.
London, 22 July, 1675.

LETTER XIX.
SPINOZA TO OLDENBURG.

[Spinoza relates his journey to Amsterdam for the purpose of publishing his Ethics; he was deterred by the dissuasions of theologians and Cartesians. He hopes that Oldenburg will inform him of some of the objections to the Tractatus Theologico-Politicos, made by learned men, so that they may be answered in notes.]

Distinguished and Illustrious Sir,—When I received your letter of the 22nd July, I had set out to Amsterdam for the purpose of publishing the book I had mentioned to you. While I was negotiating, a rumour gained currency that I had in the press a book concerning God, wherein I endeavoured to show that there is no God. This report was believed by many. Hence certain theologians, perhaps the authors of the rumour, took occasion to complain of me before the prince and the magistrates; moreover, the stupid Cartesians, being suspected of favouring me, endeavoured to remove the aspersion by abusing everywhere my opinions and writings, a course which they still pursue. When I became aware of this through trustworthy men, who also assured me that the theologians were everywhere lying in wait for me, I determined to put off publishing till I saw how things were going, and I proposed to inform you of my intentions. But matters seem to get worse and worse, and I am still uncertain what to do. Meanwhile I do not like to delay any longer answering your letter. I will first thank you heartily for your friendly warning, which I should be glad to have further explained, so that I may know, which are the doctrines which seem to you to be aimed against the practice of religion and virtue. If principles agree with reason, they are, I take it, also most serviceable to virtue. Further, if it be not troubling you too much I beg you to point out the passages in the Tractatus Theologico-Politicus which are objected to by the learned, for I want to illustrate that treatise with notes, and to remove if possible the prejudices conceived against it. Farewell.

LETTER XX.
OLDENBURG TO SPINOZA.

As I see from your last letter, the book you propose to publish is in peril. It is impossible not to approve your purpose of illustrating and softening down those passages in the Tractatus Theologico-Politicus, which have given pain to its readers. First I would call attention to the ambiguities in your treatment of God and Nature: a great many people think you have confused the one with the other. Again, you seem to many to take away the authority and value of miracles, whereby alone, as nearly all Christians believe, the certainty of the divine revelation can be established.

Again, people say that you conceal your opinion concerning Jesus Christ, the Redeemer of the world, the only Mediator for mankind, and concerning His incarnation and redemption: they would like you to give a clear explanation of what you think on these three subjects. If you do this and thus give satisfaction to prudent and rational Christians, I think your affairs are safe. Farewell.

London, 15 Nov., 1675.

P.S.—Send me a line, I beg, to inform me whether this note has reached you safely.

LETTER XXI.
SPINOZA TO OLDENBURG.

Distinguished Sir,—I received on Saturday last your very short letter dated 15th Nov. In it you merely indicate the points in the theological treatise, which have given pain to readers, whereas I had hoped to learn from it, what were the opinions which militated against the practice of religious virtue, and which you formerly mentioned. However, I will speak on the three subjects on which you desire me to disclose my sentiments, and tell you, first, that my opinion concerning God differs widely from that which is ordinarily defended by modern Christians. For I hold that God is of all things the cause immanent, as the phrase is, not transient. I say that all things are in God and move in God, thus agreeing with Paul, 1 and, perhaps, with all the ancient philosophers, though the phraseology may be different; I will even venture to affirm that I agree with all the ancient Hebrews, in so far as one may judge from their traditions, though these are in many ways corrupted. The supposition of some, that I endeavour to prove in the Tractatus Theologico-Politicos the unity of God and Nature (meaning by the latter a certain mass or corporeal matter), is wholly erroneous.

As regards miracles, I am of opinion that the revelation of God can only be established by the wisdom of the doctrine, not by miracles, or in other words by ignorance. This I have shown at sufficient length in Chapter VI. concerning miracles. I will here only add, that I make this chief distinction between religion and superstition, that the latter is founded on ignorance, the former on knowledge; this, I take it, is the reason why Christians are distinguished from the rest of the world, not by faith, nor by charity, nor by the other fruits of the Holy Spirit, but solely by their opinions, inasmuch as they defend their cause, like everyone else, by miracles, that is by ignorance, which is the source of all malice; thus they turn a faith, which may be true, into superstition. Lastly, in order to disclose my opinions on the third point, I will tell you that I do not think it necessary for salvation to know Christ according to the flesh: but with regard to the Eternal Son of God, that is the Eternal Wisdom of God, which has manifested itself in all things and especially in the human mind, and above all in Christ Jesus, the case is far otherwise. For without this no one can come to a state of blessedness, inasmuch as it alone teaches, what is true or false, good or evil. And, inasmuch as this wisdom was made especially manifest through Jesus Christ, as I have said, His disciples preached it, in so far as it was revealed to them through Him, and thus showed that they could rejoice in that spirit of Christ more than the rest of mankind. The doctrines added by certain churches, such as that God took upon Himself human nature, I have expressly said that I do not understand; in fact, to speak the truth, they seem to me no less absurd than would a statement, that a circle had taken upon itself the nature of a square. This I think will be sufficient explanation of my opinions concerning the three points mentioned. Whether it will be satisfactory to Christians you will know better than I. Farewell.

LETTER XXII.
OLDENBURG TO SPINOZA.

"[Oldenburg wishes to be enlightened concerning the doctrine of fatalism, of which Spinoza has been accused. He discourses on man's limited intelligence and on the incarnation of the Son of God.]

As you seem to accuse me of excessive brevity, I will this time avoid the charge by excessive prolixity. You expected,
see, that I should set forth those opinions in your writings, which seem to discourage the practice of religious virtue in your readers. I will indicate the matter which especially pains them. You appear to setup a fatalistic necessity for all things and actions; if such is conceded and asserted, people aver, that the sinews of all laws, of virtue, and of religion, are severed, and that all rewards and punishment are vain. Whatsoever can compel, or involves necessity, is held also to excuse; therefore no one, they think, can be without excuse in the sight of God. If we are driven by fate, and all things follow a fixed and inevitable path laid down by the hard hand of necessity, they do not see where punishment can come in. What wedge can be brought for the untying of this knot, it is very difficult to say. I should much like to know and learn what help you can supply in the matter.

As to the opinions which you have kindly disclosed to me on the three points I mentioned, the following inquiries suggest themselves. First, In what sense do you take miracles and ignorance to be synonymous and equivalent terms, as you appear to think in your last letter?

The bringing back of Lazarus from the dead, and the resurrection from death of Jesus Christ seem to surpass all the power of created nature, and to fall within the scope of divine power only; it would not be a sign of culpable ignorance, that it was necessary to exceed the limits of finite intelligence confined within certain bounds. But perhaps you do not think it in harmony with the created mind and science, to acknowledge in the uncreated mind and supreme Deity a science and power capable of fathoming, and bringing to pass events, whose reason and manner can neither be brought home nor explained to us poor human pigmies? "We are men;" it appears, that we must " think everything human akin to ourselves." 1

Again, when you say that you cannot understand that God really took upon Himself human nature, it becomes allowable to ask you, how you understand the texts in the Gospel and the Epistle to the Hebrews, whereof the first says, "The Word was made flesh," 2 and the other, "For verily he took not on him the nature of angels; but he took on him the seed of Abraham." 3 Moreover, the whole tenor of the Gospel infers, as I think, that the only begotten Son of God, the Word (who both was God and was with God), showed Himself in human nature, and by His passion and death offered up the sacrifice for our sins, the price of the atonement. What you have to say concerning this without impugning the truth of the Gospel and the Christian religion, which I think you approve of, I would gladly learn.

I had meant to write more, but am interrupted by friends on a visit, to whom I cannot refuse the duties of courtesy. But what I have already put on paper is enough, and will perhaps weary you in your philosophizing. Farewell, therefore, and believe me to be ever an admirer of your learning and knowledge.

London, 16 Dec., 1675.

LETTER XXIII.
SPINOZA TO OLDENBURG.

[Spinoza expounds to Oldenburg his views on fate and necessity, discriminates between miracles and ignorance, takes the resurrection of Christ as spiritual, and deprecates attributing to the sacred writers Western modes of speech.]

Distinguished Sir,—At last I see, what it was that you begged me not to publish. However, as it forms the chief foundation of everything in the treatise which I intended to bring out, I should like briefly to explain here, in what sense I assert that a fatal necessity presides over all things and actions. God I in no wise subject to fate: I conceive that all things follow with inevitable necessity from the nature of God, in the same way as everyone conceives that it follows from God's nature that God understands Himself. This latter consequence all admit to follow necessarily from the divine nature, yet no one conceives that God is under the compulsion of any fate, but that He understands Himself quite freely, though necessarily.

Further, this inevitable necessity in things does away neither with divine nor human laws. The principles of morality, whether they receive from God Himself the form of laws or institutions, or whether they do not, are still divine and salutary; whether we receive the good, which flows from virtue and the divine love, as from God in the capacity of a judge, or as from the necessity of the divine nature, it will in either case be equally desirable; on the other hand, the evils following from wicked actions and passions are not less to be feared because they are necessary consequences. Lastly, in our actions, whether they be necessary or contingent, we are led by hope and fear.

Men are only without excuse before God, because they are in God's power, as clay is in the hands of the potter, who from the same lump makes vessels, some to honour, some to dishonour. 1 If you will reflect a little on this, you will, I doubt not, easily be able to reply to any objections which may be urged against my opinion, as many of my friends have already done.

I have taken miracles and ignorance as equivalent terms, because those, who endeavour to establish God's existence and the truth of religion by means of miracles, seek to prove the obscure by what is more obscure and completely unknown, thus introducing a new sort of argument, the reduction, not to the impossible, as the phrase is, but to ignorance. But, if I mistake not, I have sufficiently explained my opinion on miracles in the Theologico-Political treatise. I will only add here, that if you will reflect on the facts that Christ did not appear to the council, nor to Pilate, nor to any unbeliever, but only to the faithful,; also that God has neither right hand nor left, but is by His essence not in a particular spot, but everywhere that matter is every where the same; that God does not manifest himself in the imaginary space supposed to be outside the world; and lastly, that the frame of the human body is kept within due limits solely by the weight of the air; you will readily see that this apparition of Christ is not unlike that wherewith God appeared to Abraham, when the latter saw men whom he invited to dine with him. But, you will say, all the Apostles thoroughly believed, that Christ rose from the dead and really ascended to heaven: I do not deny it. Abraham, too, believed that God had dined with him, and all the Israelites believed that God descended, surrounded with fire, from heaven to Mount Sinai, and there spoke directly with them; whereas, these apparitions or revelations, and many others like them, were adapted to the understanding and opinions of those men, to whom God wished thereby to reveal His will. I therefore conclude, that the resurrection of Christ from the dead was in reality spiritual, and that to the faithful alone, according to their understanding, it was revealed that Christ was endowed with eternity, and had risen from the dead (using dead in the sense in which Christ said, "let the dead bury their dead" 1), giving by His life and death a matchless example of holiness. Moreover, He to this extent raises his disciples from the dead, in so far as they follow the example of His own life and death. It would not be difficult to explain the whole Gospel doctrine on this hypothesis. Nay, 1 Cor. ch. xv. cannot be explained on any other, nor can Paul's arguments be understood: if we follow the common interpretation, they appear weak and can easily be refuted: not to mention the fact, that Christians interpret spiritually all those doctrines which the Jews accepted literally. I join with you in acknowledging human weakness. But on the other hand, I venture to ask you whether we "human pigmies" possess sufficient knowledge of nature to be able to lay down the limits of its force and power, or to say that a given thing surpasses that power? No one could go so far without arrogance. We may, therefore, without presumption explain miracles as far as possible by natural causes. When we cannot explain them, nor even prove their impossibility, we may well suspend our judgment about them, and establish religion, as I have said, solely by the wisdom of its doctrines. You think that the texts in John's Gospel and in Hebrews are inconsistent with what I advance, because you measure oriental phrases by the standards of European speech; though John wrote his gospel in Greek, he wrote it as a Hebrew. However this may be, do you believe, when Scripture says that God manifested Himself in a cloud, or that He dwelt in the tabernacle or the temple, that God actually assumed the nature of a cloud, a tabernacle, or a temple? Yet the utmost that Christ says of Himself is, that He is the Temple of God, 1 because, as I said before, God had specially manifested Himself in Christ. John, wishing to express the same truth more forcibly, said that "the Word was made flesh." But I have said enough on the subject.

LETTER XXIV.
OLDENBURG TO SPINOZA.

[Oldenburg returns to the questions of universal necessity, of miracles, and of the literal and allegorical interpretation of Scripture.]

You hit the point exactly, in perceiving the cause why I did not wish the doctrine of the fatalistic necessity of all things to be promulgated, lest the practice of virtue should thereby be aspersed, and rewards and punishments become ineffectual. The suggestions in your last letter hardly seem sufficient to settle the matter, or to quiet the human mind. For if we men are, in all our actions, moral as well as natural, under the power of God, like clay in the hands of the potter, with what face can any of us be accused of doing this or that, seeing that it was impossible for him to do otherwise? Should we not be able to cast all responsibility on God? Your inflexible fate, and your irresistible power, compel us to act in a given manner, nor can we possibly act otherwise. Why, then, and by what right do you deliver us up to terrible punishments, which we can in no way avoid, since you direct and carry on all things through supreme necessity, according to your good will and pleasure? When you say that men are only inexcusable before God, because they are in the power of God, I should reverse the argument, and say, with more show of reason, that men are evidently excusable, since they are in the power of God. Everyone may plead, "Thy power cannot be escaped from, O God; therefore, since I could not act otherwise, I may justly be excused."

Again, in taking miracles and ignorance as equivalent terms, you seem to bring within the same limits the power of God and the knowledge of the ablest men; for God is, according to you, unable to do or produce anything, for which men cannot assign a reason, if they employ all the strength of their faculties.

Again, the history of Christ's passion, death, burial, and resurrection seems to be depicted in such lively and genuine colours, that I venture to appeal to your conscience, whether you can believe them to be allegorical, rather than literal, while preserving your faith in the narrative? The circumstances so clearly stated by the Evangelists seem to urge strongly on our minds, that the history should be understood literally. I have ventured to touch briefly on these points, and I earnestly beg you to pardon me, and answer me as a friend with your usual candour. Mr. Boyle sends you his kind regards. I will, another time, tell you what the Royal Society is doing. Farewell, and preserve me in your affection.

London, 14 Jan., 1676.

LETTER XXV.
Written 7 Feb., 1676.
SPINOZA TO OLDENBURG.

[Spinoza again treats of fatalism. He repeats that he accepts Christ's passion, death, and burial literally, but His resurrection spiritually.]

Distinguished Sir,—When I said in my former letter that we are inexcusable, because we are in the power of God, like clay in the hands of the potter, I meant to be understood in the sense, that no one can bring a complaint against God for having given him a weak nature, or infirm spirit. A circle might as well complain to God of not being endowed with the properties of a sphere, or a child who is tortured, say, with stone, for not being given a healthy body, as a man of feeble spirit, because God has denied to him fortitude, and the true knowledge and love of the Deity, or because he is endowed with so weak a nature, that he cannot check or moderate his desires. For the nature of each thing is only competent to do that which follows necessarily from its given cause. That every man cannot be brave, and that we can no more command for ourselves a healthy body than a healthy mind, nobody can deny, without giving the lie to experience, as well as to reason. "But," you urge, "if men sin by nature, they are excusable;" but you do not state the conclusion you draw, whether that God cannot be angry with them, or that they are worthy of blessedness—that is, of the knowledge and love of God. If you say the former, I fully admit that God cannot be angry, and that all things are done in accordance with His will; but I deny that all men ought, therefore, to be blessed—men may be excusable, and, nevertheless, be without blessedness and afflicted in many ways. A horse is excusable, for being a horse and not a man; but, nevertheless, he must needs be a horse and not a man. He who goes mad from the bite of a dog is excusable, yet he is rightly suffocated. Lastly, he who cannot govern his desires, and keep them in check with the fear of the laws, though his weakness may be excusable, yet he cannot enjoy with contentment the knowledge and love of God, but necessarily perishes. I do not think it necessary here to remind you, that Scripture, when it says that God is angry with sinners, and that He is a Judge who takes cognizance of human actions, passes sentence on them, and judges them, is speaking humanly, and in a way adapted to the received opinion of the masses, inasmuch as its purpose is not to teach philosophy, nor to render men wise, but to make them obedient.

How, by taking miracles and ignorance as equivalent terms, I reduce God's power and man's knowledge within the same limits, I am unable to discern.

For the rest, I accept Christ's passion, death, and burial literally, as you do, but His resurrection I understand allegorically. I admit, that it is related by the Evangelists in such detail, that we cannot deny that they themselves believed

Christ's body to have risen from the dead and ascended to heaven, in order to sit at the right hand of God, or that they believed that Christ might have been seen by unbelievers, if they had happened to be at hand, in the places where He appeared to His disciples; but in these matters they might, without injury to Gospel teaching, have been deceived, as was the case with other prophets mentioned in my last letter. But Paul, to whom Christ afterwards appeared, rejoices, that he knew Christ not after the flesh, but after the spirit. 1 Farewell, honourable Sir, and believe me yours in all affection and zeal.

LETTER XXV.A.
OLDENBURG TO SPINOZA.

[Oldenburg adduces certain further objections against Spinoza's doctrine of necessity and miracles, and exposes the inconsistency of a partial allegorization of Scripture.]

To the most illustrious Master Benedict de Spinoza Henry Oldenburg sends greetings.

In your last letter, 2 written to me on the 7th of February, there are some points which seem to deserve criticism. You say that a man cannot complain, because God has denied him the true knowledge of Himself, and strength sufficient to avoid sins; forasmuch as to the nature of everything nothing is competent, except that which follows necessarily from its cause. But I say, that inasmuch as God, the creator of men, formed them after His own image, which seems to imply in its concept wisdom, goodness, and power, it appears quite to follow, that it is more within the sphere of man's power 3 to have a sound mind than to have a sound body. For physical soundness of body follows from mechanical causes, but soundness of mind depends on purpose and design. You add, that men may be inexcusable, 1 and yet suffer pain in many ways. This seems hard at first sight, and what you add by way of proof, namely, that a dog 2 mad from having been bitten is indeed to be excused, but yet is rightly killed, does not seem to settle the question. For the killing of such a dog would argue cruelty, were it not necessary in order to preserve other dogs and animals, and indeed men, from a maddening bite of the same kind.

But if God implanted in man a sound mind, as He is able to do, there would be no contagion of vices to be feared. And, surely, it seems very cruel, that God should de. vote men to eternal, or at least terrible temporary, torments, for sins which by them could be no wise avoided. Moreover, the tenour of all Holy Scripture seems to suppose and imply, that men can abstain from sins. For it abounds in denunciations and promises, in declarations of rewards and punishments, all of which seem to militate against the necessity of sinning, and infer the possibility of avoiding punishment. And if this were denied, it would have to be said, that the human mind acts no less mechanically than the human body.

Next, when you proceed to take miracles and ignorance to be equivalent, you seem to rely on this foundation, that the creature can and should have perfect insight into the power and wisdom of the Creator: and that the fact is quite otherwise, I have hitherto been firmly persuaded.

Lastly, where you affirm that Christ's passion, death, and burial are to be taken literally, but His resurrection allegorically, you rely, as far as I can see, on no proof at all. Christ's resurrection seems to be delivered in the Gospel as literally as the rest. And on this article of the resurrection the whole Christian religion and its truth rest, and with its removal Christ's mission and heavenly doctrine collapse. It cannot escape you, how Christ, after He was raised from the dead, laboured to convince His disciples of the truth of the Resurrection properly so called. To want to turn all these things into allegories is the same thing, as if one were to busy one's self in plucking up the whole truth of the Gospel history.

These few points I wished again to submit in the interest of my liberty of philosophizing, which I earnestly beg you not to take amiss.

Written in London, 11 Feb., 1676.

I will communicate with you shortly on the present studies and experiments of the Royal Society, if God grant me life and health.

LETTER XXVI.
SIMON DE VRIES 1 TO SPINOZA.

[Simon de Vries, a diligent student of Spinoza's writings and philosophy, describes a club formed for the study of Spinoza's MS. containing some of the matter afterwards worked into the Ethics, and asks questions about the difficulties felt by members of the club.]

Most Honourable Friend,—I have for a long time wished to be present with you; but the weather and the hard winter have not been propitious to me. I sometimes complain of my lot, in that we are separated from each other by so long a distance. Happy, yes most happy is the fellow-lodger, abiding under the same roof with you, who can talk with you on the best of subjects, at dinner, at supper, and during your walks. 1 However, though I am far apart from you in body, you have been very frequently present to my mind, especially in your writings, while I read and turn them over. But as they are not all clear to the members of our club, for which reason we have begun a fresh series of meetings, and as I would not have you think me unmindful of you, I have applied my mind to writing this letter.

As regards our club, the following is its order. One of us (that is everyone by turn) reads through and, as far as he understands it, expounds and also demonstrates the whole of your work, according to the sequence and order of your propositions. Then, if it happens that on any point we cannot satisfy one another, we have resolved to make a note of it and write to you, so that, if possible, it may be made clearer to us, and that we may be able under your guidance to defend the truth against those who are superstitiously religious, and against the Christians, 2 and to withstand the attack of the whole world. Well then, since, when we first read through and expounded them, the definitions did not all seem clear to us, we differed about the nature of definition. Next in your absence we consulted as our authority a celebrated mathematician, named Borel: 3 for he makes mention of the nature of definition, axiom, and postulate, and adduces the opinions of others on the subject. But his opinion is as follows: "Definitions are cited in a demonstration as premises. Wherefore it is necessary, that they should be accurately known; otherwise scientific or accurate knowledge cannot be attained by their means." And elsewhere he says: "The primary and most known construction or passive quality of a given subject should not be chosen rashly, but with the greatest care; if the construction or passive quality be an impossibility, no scientific definition can be obtained. For instance, if anyone were to say, let two straight lines enclosing a space be called figurals, the definition would be of non-existences and impossible: hence ignorance rather than knowledge would be deduced therefrom. Again, if the construction or passive quality be possible and true, but unknown or doubtful to us, the definition will not be good. For conclusions arising from what is unknown or doubtful are themselves uncertain or doubtful; they therefore bring about conjecture or opinion, but not certain knowledge.

Jacquet 1 seems to dissent from this opinion, for he thinks that one may proceed from a false premiss directly to true conclusion, as you are aware. Clavius, 2 however, whose opinion he quotes, thinks as follows: "Definitions," he says, "are artificial phrases, nor is there any need in reasoning that a thing should be defined in a particular way; but it is sufficient that a thing defined should never be said to agree with another thing, until it has been shown that its definition also agrees therewith."

Thus, according to Borel, the definition of a given thing should consist as regards its construction or passive quality in something thoroughly known to us and true. Clavius, on the other hand, holds that it is a matter of indifference, whether the construction or passive quality be well known and true, or the reverse; so long as we do not assert, that our definition agrees with anything, before it has been proved.

I should prefer Borers opinion to that of Clavius. I know not which you would assent to, if to either. As these difficulties have occurred to me with regard to the nature of definition, which is reckoned among the cardinal points of demonstration, and as I cannot free my mind from them, I greatly desire, and earnestly beg you, when you have leisure and opportunity, to be kind enough to send me your opinion on the matter, and at the same time to tell me the distinction between axioms and definitions. Borel says that the difference is merely nominal, but I believe you decide otherwise.

Further, we cannot make up our minds about the third definition. 1 I adduced to illustrate it, what my master said to me at the Hague, 2 to wit, that a thing may be regarded in two ways, either as it is in itself, or as it is in relation to something else; as in the case of the intellect, for that can be regarded either under the head of thought, or as consisting in ideas. But we do not see the point of the distinction thus drawn. For it seems to us, that, if we rightly conceive thought, we must range it under the head of ideas; as, if all ideas were removed from it, we should destroy thought. As we find the illustration of the matter not sufficiently clear, the matter itself remains somewhat obscure, and we need further explanation.

Lastly, in the third note to the eighth proposition, 3 the beginning runs thus:—"Hence it is plain that, although two attributes really distinct be conceived, that is, one without the aid of the other, we cannot therefore infer, that they constitute two entities or two different substances. For it belongs to the nature of substance, that each of its attributes should be conceived through itself, though all the attributes it possesses exist simultaneously in it." Here our master seems to assume, that the nature of substance is so constituted, that it may have several attributes. But this doctrine has not yet been proved, unless you refer to the sixth definition, of absolutely infinite substance or God. Otherwise, if it be asserted that each substance has only one attribute, and I have two ideas of two attributes, Î may rightly infer that, where there are two different attributes, there are also different substances. On this point also we beg you to give a further explanation. Besides I thank you very much for your writings communicated to me by P. Balling, 4 which have greatly delighted me, especially your note on Proposition XIX. 1 If I can do you any service here in anything that is within my power, I am at your disposal. You have but to let me know. I have begun a course of anatomy, and am nearly half through with it; when it is finished, I shall begin a course of chemistry, and thus under your guidance I shall go through the whole of medicine. I leave off, and await your answer. Accept the greeting of

Your most devoted

S. J. DE VRIES.

Amsterdam, 24 Feb., 1663.

LETTER XXVII.
SPINOZA TO SIMON DE VRIES.

[Spinoza deprecates his correspondent's jealousy of Albert Burgh; and answers that distinction must be made between different kinds of definitions. He explains his opinions more precisely.]

Respected Friend,—I have received 2 your long wished-for letter, for which, and for your affection towards me, I heartily thank you. Your long absence has been no less grievous to me than to you; yet in the meantime I rejoice that my trifling studies are of profit to you and our friends. For thus while you 3 are away, I in my absence speak to you. 3 You need not envy my fellow-lodger. There is no one who is more displeasing to me, nor against whom I have been more anxiously on my guard; and therefore I would have you and all my acquaintance warned not to communicate my opinions to him,—except when he has come to maturer years. So far he is too childish and inconstant, and is fonder of novelty than of truth. But I hope, that in a few years he will amend these childish faults. Indeed I am almost sure of it, as far as I can judge from his nature. And so his temperament bids me like him.

As for the questions propounded in your club, which is wisely enough ordered, I see that your 1 difficulties arise from not distinguishing between kinds of definition: that is, between a definition serving to explain a thing, of which the essence only is sought and in question, and a definition which is put forward only for purposes of inquiry. The former having a definite object ought to be true, the latter need not. For instance, if someone asks me for a description of Solomon's temple, I am bound to give him a true description, unless I want to talk nonsense with him. But if I have constructed, in my mind, a temple which I desire to build, and infer from the description of it that I must buy such and such a site and so many thousand stones and other materials, will any sane person tell me that I have drawn a wrong conclusion because my definition is possibly untrue? or will anyone ask me to prove my definition? Such a person would simply be telling me, that I had not conceived that which I had conceived, or be requiring me to prove, that I had conceived that which I had conceived; in fact, evidently trifling. Hence a definition either explains a thing, in so far as it is external to the intellect, in which case it ought to be true and only to differ from a proposition or an axiom in being concerned merely with the essences of things, or the modifications of things, whereas the latter has a wider scope and extends also to eternal truths. Or else it explains a thing, as it is conceived or can be conceived by us; and then it differs from an axiom or proposition, inasmuch as it only requires to be conceived absolutely, and not like an axiom as true. Hence a bad definition is one which is not conceived. To explain my meaning, I will take Borel's example—a man saying that two straight lines enclosing a space shall be called "figurals." If the man means by a straight line the same as the rest of the world means by a curved line, his definition is good (for by the definition would be meant some such figure as (), or the like); so long as he does not afterwards mean a square or other kind of figure. But, if he attaches the ordinary meaning to the words straight line, the thing is evidently inconceivable, and therefore there is no definition. These considerations are plainly confused by Borel, to whose opinion you incline. I give another example, the one you cite at the end of your letter. If I say that each substance has only one attribute, this is an unsupported statement and needs proof. But, if I say that I mean by substance that which consists in only one attribute, the definition will be good, so long as entities consisting of several attributes are afterwards styled by some name other than substance. When you say that I do not prove, that substance (or being) may have several attributes, you do not perhaps pay attention to the proofs given. I adduced two:—First, "that nothing is plainer to us, than that every being may be conceived by us under some attribute, and that the more reality or essence a given being has, the more attributes may be attributed to it. Hence a being absolutely infinite must be defined, &c." Secondly, and I think this is the stronger proof of the two, "the more attributes I assign to any being, the more am I compelled to assign to it existence;" in other words, the more I conceive it as true. The contrary would evidently result, if I were feigning a chimera or some such being.

Your remark, that you cannot conceive thought except as consisting in ideas, because, when ideas are removed, thought is annihilated, springs, I think, from the fact that while you, a thinking thing, do as you say, you abstract all your thoughts and conceptions. It is no marvel that, when you have abstracted all your thoughts and conceptions, you have nothing left for thinking with. On the general subject I think I have shown sufficiently clearly and plainly, that the intellect, although infinite, belongs to nature regarded as passive rather than nature regarded as active (ad naturam naturatam, non vero ad naturam naturantem).

However, I do not see how this helps towards understanding the third definition, nor what difficulty the latter presents. It runs, if I mistake not, as follows: "By substance I mean that, which is in itself and is conceived through itself; that is, of which the conception does not involve the conception of anything else. By attribute I mean the same thing, except that it is called attribute with respect to the understanding, which attributes to substance the particular nature aforesaid." This definition, I repeat, explains with sufficient clearness what I wish to signify by substance or attribute. You desire, though there is no need, that I should illustrate by an example, how one and the same thing can be stamped with two names. In order not to seem miserly, I will give you two. First, I say that by Israel is meant the third patriarch; I mean the same by Jacob, the name Jacob being given, because the patriarch in question had caught hold of the heel of his brother. Secondly, by a colourless surface I mean a surface, which reflects all rays of light without altering them. I mean the same by a white surface, with this difference, that a surface is called white in reference to a man looking at it, &c.

LETTER XXVIII.
SPINOZA TO SIMON DE VRIES.

[Spinoza, in answer to a letter from De Vries now lost, speaks of the experience necessary for proving a definition, and also of eternal truths.]

Respected Friend,—You ask me if we have need of experience, in order to know whether the definition of a given attribute is true. To this I answer, that we never need experience, except in cases when the existence of the thing cannot be inferred from its definition, as, for instance, the existence of modes (which cannot be inferred from their definition); experience is not needed, when the existence of the things in question is not distinguished from their essence, and is therefore inferred from their definition. This can never be taught us by any experience, for experience does not teach us any essences of things; the utmost it can do is to set our mind thinking about definite essences only. Wherefore, when the existence of attributes does not differ from their essence, no experience is capable of attaining it for us.

To your further question, whether things and their modifications are eternal truths, I answer: Certainly. If you ask me, why I do not call them eternal truths, I answer, in order to distinguish them, in accordance with general usage, from those propositions, which do not make manifest any particular thing or modification of a thing; for example, nothing comes from nothing. These and such like propositions are, I repeat, called eternal truths simply, the meaning merely being, that they have no standpoint external to the mind, &c.

LETTER XXIX.
SPINOZA TO L. M. 1 (LEWIS MEYER).

Dearest Friend,—I have received two letters from you, one dated Jan. 11, delivered to me by our friend, N. N., the other dated March 26, sent by some unknown friend to Leyden. They were both most welcome to me, especially as I gathered from them, that all goes well with you, and that you are often mindful of me. I also owe and repay you the warmest thanks for the courtesy and consideration, with which you have always been kind enough to treat me: I hope you will believe, that I am in no less degree devoted to you, as, when occasion offers, I will always endeavour to prove, as far as my poor powers will admit. As a first proof, I will do my best to answer the questions you ask in your letters. You request me to tell you, what I think about the infinite; I will most readily do so.

Everyone regards the question of the infinite as most difficult, if not insoluble, through not making a distinction between that which must be infinite from its very nature,. or in virtue of its definition, and that which has no limits, not in virtue of its essence, but in virtue of its cause; and also through not distinguishing between that which is called infinite, because it has no limits, and that, of which the parts cannot be equalled or expressed by any number, though the greatest and least magnitude of the whole may be known; and, lastly, through not distinguishing between that, which can be understood but not imagined, and that which can also be imagined. If these distinctions, I repeat, had been attended to, inquirers would not have been overwhelmed with such a vast crowd of difficulties. They would then clearly have understood, what kind of infinite is indivisible and possesses no parts; and what kind, on the other hand, may be divided without involving a contradiction in terms. They would further have understood, what kind of infinite may, without solecism, be conceived greater than another infinite, and what kind cannot be so conceived. All this will plainly appear from what I am about to say.

However, I will first briefly explain the terms substance, mode, eternity, and duration.

The points to be noted concerning substance are these: First, that existence appertains to its essence; in other words, that solely from its essence and definition its existence follows. This, if I remember rightly, I have already proved to you by word of mouth, without the aid of any other propositions. Secondly, as a consequence of the above, that substance is not manifold, but single: there cannot be two of the same nature. Thirdly, every substance must be conceived as infinite.

The modifications of substance I call modes. Their definition, in so far as it is not identical with that of substance, cannot involve any existence. Hence, though they exist, we can conceive them as non-existent. From this it follows, that, when we are regarding only the essence of modes, and not the order of the whole of nature, we cannot conclude from their present existence, that they will exist or not exist in the future, or that they have existed or not existed in the past; whence it is abundantly clear, that we conceive the existence of substance as entirely different from the existence of modes. From this difference arises the distinction between eternity and duration. Duration is only applicable to the existence of modes; eternity is applicable to the existence of substance. that is, the infinite faculty of existence or being (infinitum existendi sive (invitâ Latinitate 1) essendi fruitionem). From what has been said it is quite clear that, when, as is most often the case, we are regarding only the essence of modes and not the order of nature, we may freely limit the existence and duration of modes without destroying the conception we have formed of them; we may conceive them as greater or less, or may divide them into parts. Eternity and substance, being only conceivable as infinite, cannot be thus treated without our conception of them being destroyed. Wherefore it is mere foolishness, or even insanity, to say that extended substance is made up of parts or bodies really distinct from one another. It is as though one should attempt by the aggregation and addition of many circles to make up a square, or a triangle, or something of totally different essence. Wherefore the whole heap of arguments, by which philosophers commonly en' to show that extended substance is finite, falls to the ground by its own weight. For all such persons suppose, that corporeal substance is made up of parts. In the same way, others, who have persuaded themselves that a line is made up of points, have been able to discover many arguments to show that a line is not infinitely divisible. If you ask, why we are by nature so prone to attempt to divide extended substance, I answer, that quantity is conceived by us in two ways, namely, by abstraction or superficially, as we imagine it by the aid of the senses, or as substance, which can only be accomplished through the understanding. So that, if we regard quantity as it exists in the imagination (and this is the more frequent and easy method), it will be found to be divisible, finite, composed of parts, and manifold. But, if we regard it as it is in the understanding, and the thing be conceived as it is in itself (which is very difficult), it will then, as I have sufficiently shown you before, be found to be infinite, indivisible, and single.

Again, from the fact that we can limit duration and quantity at our pleasure, when we conceive the latter abstractedly as apart from substance, and separate the former from the manner whereby it flows from things eternal, there arise time and measure; time for the purpose of limiting duration, measure for the purpose of limiting quantity, so that we may, as far as is possible, the more readily imagine them. Further, inasmuch as we separate the modifications of substance from substance itself, and reduce them to classes, so that we may, as far as is possible, the more readily imagine them, there arises number, whereby we limit them. Whence it is clearly to be seen, that measure, time, and number, are merely modes of thinking, or, rather, of imagining. It is not to be wondered at, therefore, that all, who have endeavoured to understand the course of nature by means of such notions, and without fully understanding even them, have entangled themselves so wondrously, that they have at last only been able to extricate themselves by breaking through every rule and admitting absurdities even of the grossest kind. For there are many things which cannot be conceived through the imagination but only through the understanding, for instance, substance, eternity, and the like; thus, if anyone tries to explain such things by means of conceptions which are mere aids to the imagination, he is simply assisting his imagination to run away with him. 1 Nor can even the modes of substance ever be rightly understood, if we confuse them with entities of the kind mentioned, mere aids of the reason or imagination. In so doing we separate them from substance, and the mode of their derivation from eternity, without which they can never be rightly understood. To make the matter yet more clear, take the following example: when a man conceives of duration abstractedly, and, confusing it with time, begins to divide it into parts, he will never be able to understand how an hour, for instance, can elapse. For in order that an hour should elapse, it is necessary that its half should elapse first, and afterwards half of the remainder, and again half of the half of the remainder, and if you go on thus to infinity, subtracting the half of the residue, you will never be able to arrive at the end of the hour. Wherefore many, who are not accustomed to distinguish abstractions from realities, have ventured to assert that duration is made up of instants, and so in wishing to avoid Charybdis have fallen into Scylla. It is the same thing to make up duration out of instants, as it is to make number simply by adding up noughts.

Further, as it is evident from what has been said, that neither number, nor measure, nor time, being mere aids to the imagination, can be infinite (for, otherwise, number would not be number, nor measure measure, nor time time); it is hence abundantly evident, why many who confuse these three abstractions with realities, through being ignorant of the true nature of things, have actually denied the infinite.

The wretchedness of their reasoning may be judged by mathematicians, who have never allowed themselves to be delayed a moment by arguments of this sort, in the case of things which they clearly and distinctly perceive. For not only have they come across many things, which cannot be expressed by number (thus showing the inadequacy of number for determining all things); but also they have found many things, which cannot be equalled by any number, but surpass every possible number. But they infer hence, that such things surpass enumeration, not because of the multitude of their component parts, but because their nature cannot, without manifest contradiction, be expressed in terms of number. As, for instance, in the case of two circles, non-concentric, whereof one encloses the other, no number can express the inequalities of distance which exist between the two circles, nor all the variations which matter in motion in the intervening space may undergo. This conclusion is not based on the excessive size of the intervening space. However small a portion of it we take, the inequalities of this small portion will surpass all numerical expression. Nor, again, is the conclusion based on the fact, as in other cases, that we do not know the maximum and the minimum of the said space. It springs simply from the fact, that the nature of the space between two non-concentric circles cannot be expressed in number. Therefore, he who would assign a numerical equivalent for the inequalities in question, would be bound, at the same time, to bring about that a circle should not be a circle.

The same result would take place—to return to my subject—if one were to wish to determine all the motions undergone by matter up to the present, by reducing them and their duration to a certain number and time. This would be the same as an attempt to deprive corporeal substance, which we cannot conceive except as existent, of its modifications, and to bring about that it should not possess the nature which it does possess. All this I could clearly demonstrate here, together with many other points touched on in this letter, but I deem it superfluous.

From all that has been said, it is abundantly evident that certain things are in their nature infinite, and can by no means be conceived as finite; whereas there are other things, infinite in virtue of the cause from which they are derived, which can, when conceived abstractedly, be divided into parts, and regarded as finite. Lastly, there are some which are called infinite or, if you prefer, indefinite, because they cannot be expressed in number, which may yet be conceived as greater or less. It does not follow that such are equal, because they are alike incapable of numerical expression. This is plain enough, from the example given, and many others.

Lastly, I have put briefly before you the causes of error and confusion, which have arisen concerning the question of the infinite. I have, if I mistake not, so explained them that no question concerning the infinite remains untreated, or cannot readily be solved from what I have said; wherefore, I do not think it worth while to detain you longer on the matter.

But I should like it first to be observed here, that the later Peripatetics have, I think, misunderstood the proof given by the ancients who sought to demonstrate the existence of God. This, as I find it in a certain Jew named Rabbi Ghasdai, runs as follows:—"If there be an infinite series of causes, all things which are, are caused. But nothing which is caused can exist necessarily in virtue of its own nature. Therefore there is nothing in nature, to whose essence existence necessarily belongs. But this is absurd. Therefore the premise is absurd also." Hence the force of the argument lies not in the impossibility of an actual infinite or an infinite series of causes; but only in the absurdity of the assumption that things, which do not necessarily exist by nature, are not conditioned for existence by a thing, which does by its own nature necessarily exist.

I would now pass on, for time presses, to your second letter: but I shall be able more conveniently to reply to its contents, when you are kind enough to pay me a visit. I therefore beg that you will come as soon as possible; the time for travelling is at hand. Enough. Farewell, and keep in remembrance Yours, &c.

Rhijnsburg, 20 April, 1663.

LETTER XXIX.A. 1
SPINOZA TO LEWIS MEYER.

Dear Friend,—The preface you sent me by our friend De Vries, I now send back to you by the same hand. Some few things, as you will see, I have marked in the margin; but yet a few remain, which I have judged it better to mention to you by letter. First, where on page 4 you give the reader to know on what occasion I composed the first part; I would have you likewise explain there, or where you please, that I composed it within a fortnight. For when this is explained none will suppose the exposition to be so clear as that it cannot be bettered, and so they will not stick at obscurities in this and that phrase on which they may chance to stumble. Secondly, I would have you explain, that when I prove many points otherwise than they 'be proved by Descartes, 'tis not to amend Descartes, but the better to preserve my order, and not to multiply axioms overmuch: and that for this same reason I prove many things which by Descartes are barely alleged without any proof, and must needs add other matters which Descartes let alone. Lastly, I will earnestly beseech you, as my especial friend, to let be everything you have written, towards the end against that creature, and wholly strike it out. And though many reasons determine me to this request, I will give but one. I would fain have all men readily believe that these matters are published for the common profit of the world, and that your sole motive in bringing out the book is the love of spreading the truth; and that it is accordingly all your study to make the work acceptable to all, to bid men, with all courtesy to the pursuit of genuine philosophy, and to consult their common advantage. Which every man will be ready to think when he sees that no one is attacked, nor anything advanced where any man can find the least offence. Notwithstanding, if afterwards the person you know of, or any other, be minded to display his ill will, then you may portray his life and character, and gain applause by it. So I ask that you will not refuse to be patient thus far, and suffer yourself to be entreated, and believe me wholly bounden to you, and

Yours with all affection,

B. DE SPINOZA.

Voorburg, Aug. 3, 1663.

Our friend De Vries had promised to take this with him; but seeing he knows not when he will return to you, I send it by another hand.

Along with this I send you part of the scholium to Prop. xxvii. Part II. where page 75 begins, that you may hand it to the printer to be reprinted. The matter I send you must of necessity be reprinted, and fourteen or fifteen lines added, which may easily be inserted.

LETTER XXX.
SPINOZA TO PETER BALLING. 1

[Concerning omens and phantoms. The mind may have a confused presentiment of the future.]

Beloved Friend,—Your last letter, written, if I mistake not, on the 26th of last month, has duly reached me. It caused me no small sorrow and solicitude, though the feeling sensibly diminished when I reflected on the good sense and fortitude, with which you have known how to despise the evils of fortune, or rather of opinion, at a time when they most bitterly assailed you. Yet my anxiety increases daily; I therefore .beg and implore you by the claims of our friendship, that you will rouse yourself to write me a long letter. With regard to Omens, of which you make mention in telling me that, while your child was still healthy and strong, you heard groans like those he uttered when he was ill and shortly afterwards died, I should judge that these were not real groans, but only the effect of your imagination; for you say that, when you got up and composed yourself to listen, you did not hear them so clearly either as before or as afterwards, when you had fallen asleep again. This, I think, shows that the groans were purely due to the imagination, which, when it was unfettered and free, could imagine groans more forcibly and vividly than when you sat up in order to listen in a particular direction. I think I can both illustrate and confirm what I say by another occurrence, which befell me at Rhijnsburg last winter. When one morning, after the day had dawned, I woke up from a very unpleasant dream, the images, which had presented themselves to me in sleep, remained before my eyes just as vividly as though the things had been real, especially the image of a certain black and leprous Brazilian whom I had never seen before. This image disappeared for the most part when, in order to divert my thoughts, I cast my eyes on a book, or something else. But, as soon as I lifted my eyes again without fixing my attention on any particular object, the same image of this same negro appeared with the same vividness again and again, until the head of it gradually vanished. I say that the same thing, which occurred with regard to my inward sense of sight, occurred with your hearing; but as the causes were very different, your case was an omen and mine was not. The matter may be clearly grasped by means of what I am about to say. The effects of the imagination arise either from bodily or mental causes. I will proceed to prove this, in order not to be too long, solely from experience. We know that fevers and other bodily ailments are the causes of delirium, and that persons of stubborn disposition imagine nothing but quarrels, brawls, slaughterings, and the like. We also see that the imagination is to a certain extent determined by the character of the disposition, for, as we know by experience, it follows in the tracks of the understanding in every respect, and arranges its images and words, just as the understanding arranges its demonstrations and connects one with another; so that we are hardly at all able to say, what will not serve the imagination as a basis for some image or other. This being so, I say that no effects of imagination springing from physical causes can ever be omens of future events; inasmuch as their causes do not involve any future events. But the effects of imagination, or images originating in the mental disposition, may be omens of some future event; inasmuch as the mind may have a confused presentiment of the future. It may, therefore, imagine a future event as forcibly and vividly, as though it were present; for instance a father (to take an example resembling your own) loves his child so much, that he and the beloved child are, as it were, one and the same. And since (like that which I demonstrated on another occasion) there must necessarily exist in thought the idea of the essence of the child's states and their results, and since the father, through his union with his child, is a part of the said child, the soul of the father must necessarily participate in the ideal essence of the child and his states, and in their results, as I have shown at greater length elsewhere.

Again, as the soul of the father participates ideally in the consequences of his child's essence, he may (as I have said) sometimes imagine some of the said consequences as vividly as if they were present with him, provided that the following conditions are fulfilled:—I. If the occurrence in his son's career be remarkable. II. If it be capable of being readily imagined. III. If the time of its happening be not too remote. IV. If his body be sound, in respect not only of health but of freedom from every care or business which could outwardly trouble the senses. It may also assist the result, if we think of something which generally stimulates similar ideas. For instance, if while we are talking with this or that man we hear groans, it will generally happen that, when we think of the man again, the groans heard when we spoke with him will recur to our mind. This, dear friend, is my opinion on the question you ask me. I have, I confess, been very brief, but I have furnished you with material for writing to me on the first opportunity, &c.

Voorburg, 20 July, 1664.

LETTER XXXI.
WILLIAM DE BLYENBERGH 1 TO SPINOZA.

Unknown Friend and Sir,—I have already read several times with attention your treatise and its appendix recently published. I should narrate to others more becomingly than to yourself the extreme solidity I found in it, and the pleasure with which I perused it. But I am unable to conceal my feelings from you, because the more frequently I study the work with attention, the more it pleases me, and I am constantly observing something which I had not before remarked. However, I will not too loudly extol its author, lest I should seem in this letter to be a flatterer. I am aware that the gods grant all things to labour. Not to detain you too long with wondering who I ay be, and how it comes to pass that one unknown to you takes the great liberty of writing to you, I will tell you that he is a man who is impelled by his longing for pure and unadulterated truth, and desires during this brief and frail life to fix his feet in the ways of science, so far as our human faculties will allow; one who in the pursuit of truth has no goal before his eyes save truth herself; one who by his science seeks to obtain as the result of truth neither honour nor riches, but simple truth and tranquillity; one who, out of the whole circle of truths and sciences, takes delight in none more than in metaphysics, if not in all branches at any rate in some; one who places the whole delight of his life in the fact, that he can pass in the study of them his hours of ease and leisure. But no one, I rest assured, is so blessed as yourself, no one has carried his studies so far, and therefore no one has arrived at the pitch of perfection which, as I see from your work, you have attained. To add a last word, the present writer is one with whom you may gain a closer acquaintance, if you choose to attach him to you by enlightening and interpenetrating, as it were, his halting meditations.

But I return to your treatise. While I found in it many things which tickled my palate vastly, some of them proved difficult to digest. Perhaps a stranger ought not to report to you his objections, the more so as I know not whether they will meet with your approval. This is the reason for my making these prefatory remarks, and asking you, if you can find leisure in the winter evenings, and, at the same time, will be willing to answer the difficulties which I still find in your book, and to forward me the result, always under the condition that it does not interrupt any occupation of greater importance or pleasure; for I desire nothing more earnestly than to see the promise made in your book fulfilled by a more detailed exposition of your opinions. I should have communicated to you by word of mouth what I now commit to paper; but my ignorance of your address, the infectious disease, 1 and my duties here, prevented me. I must defer the pleasure for the present.

However, in order that this letter may not be quite empty, and in the hope that it will not be displeasing to you, I will ask you one question. You say in various passages in the "Principia," and in the "Metaphysical Reflections," either as your own opinion, or as explaining the philosophy of Descartes, that creation and preservation are identical (which is, indeed, so evident to those who have considered the question as to be a primary notion); secondly, that God has not only created substances, but also motions in substances—in other words, that God, by a continuous act of creation preserves, not only substances in their normal state, but also the motion and the endeavours of substances. God, for instance, not only brings about by His immediate will and working (whatever be the term employed), that the soul should last and continue in its normal state; but He is also the cause of His will determining, in some way, the movement of the soul—in other words, as God, by a continuous act of creation, brings about that things should remain in existence, so is He also the cause of the movements and endeavours existing in things. In fact, save God, there is no cause of motion. It therefore follows that God is not only the cause of the substance of mind, but also of every endeavour or motion of mind, which we call volition, as you frequently say. From this statement it seems to follow necessarily, either that there is no evil in the motion or volition of the mind, or else that God directly brings about that evil. For that which we call evil comes to pass through the soul, and, consequently, through the immediate influence and concurrence of God. For instance, the soul of Adam wishes to eat of the forbidden fruit. It follows from what has been said above, not only that Adam forms his wish through the influence of God, but also, as will presently be shown, that through that influence he forms it in that particular manner. Hence, either the act forbidden to Adam is not evil, inasmuch as God Himself not only caused the wish, but also the manner of it, or else God directly brought about at which we call evil. Neither you nor Descartes seem have solved this difficulty by saying that evil is a negative conception, and that, as such, God cannot bring it about. Whence, we may ask, came the wish to eat the forbidden fruit, or the wish of devils to be equal with God? For since (as you justly observe) the will is not something different from the mind, but is only an endeavour or movement of the mind, the concurrence of God is as necessary to it as to the mind itself. Now the concurrence of God, as I gather from your writings, is merely the determining of a thing in a particular manner through the will of God. It follows that God concurs no less in an evil wish, in so far as it is evil, than in a good wish in so far as it is good, in other words, He determines it. For the will of God being the absolute cause of all that exists, either in substance or in effort, seems to be also the primary cause of an evil wish, in so far as it is evil. Again, no exercise of volition takes place in us, that God has not known from all eternity. If we say that God does not know of a particular exercise of volition, we attribute to Him imperfection. But how could God gain knowledge of it except from His decrees? Therefore His decrees are the cause of our volitions, and hence it seems also to follow that either an evil wish is not evil, or else that God is the direct cause of the evil, and brings it about. There is no room here for the theological distinction between an act and the evil inherent in that act. For God decrees the mode of the act, no less than the act, that is, God not only decreed that Adam should eat, but also that he should necessarily eat contrary to the command given. Thus it seems on all sides to follow, either that Adam's eating contrary to the command was not an evil, or else that God Himself brought it to pass.

These, illustrious Sir, are the questions in your treatise, which I am unable, at present, to elucidate. Either alternative seems to me difficult of acceptance. However, I await a satisfactory answer from your keen judgment and learning, hoping to show you hereafter how deeply indebted I shall be to you. Be assured, illustrious Sir, that I put these questions from no other motive than the desire for truth. I am a man of leisure, not tied to any profession, gaining my living by honest trade, and devoting my spare time to questions of this sort. I humbly hope that my difficulties will not be displeasing to you. If you are minded to send an answer, as I most ardently hope, write to, &c.

WILLIAM DE BLYENBERGH.

Dordrecht, 12 Dec., 1664.

LETTER XXXII.
SPINOZA TO BLYENBERGH.

(Spinoza answers with his usual courtesy the question propounded by Blyenbergh.)

Unknown Friend,—I received, at Schiedam, on the 26th of December, your letter dated the 12th of December, enclosed in another written on the 24th of the same month. I gather from it your fervent love of truth, and your making it the aim of all your studies. This compelled me, though by no means otherwise unwilling, not only to grant your petition by answering all the questions you have sent, or may in future send, to the best of my ability, but also to impart to you everything in my power, which can conduce to further knowledge and sincere friendship. So far as in me lies, I value, above all other things out of my own control, the joining hands of friendship with men who are sincere lovers of truth. I believe that nothing in the world, of things outside our own control, brings more peace than the possibility of affectionate intercourse with such men; it is just as impossible that the love we bear them can be disturbed (inasmuch as it is founded on the desire each feels for the knowledge of truth), as that truth once perceived should not be assented to. It is, moreover, the highest and most pleasing source of happiness derivable from things not under our own control. Nothing save truth has power closely to unite different feelings and dispositions. I say nothing of the very great advantages which it brings, lest I should detain you too long on a subject which, doubtless, you know already. I have said thus much, in order to show you better how gladly I shall embrace this and any future opportunity of serving you.

In order to make the best of the present opportunity, I will at once proceed to answer your question. This seems to turn on the point "that it seems to be clear, not only from God's providence, which is identical with His will, but also from God's co-operation and continuous creation of things, either that there are no such things as sin or evil, or that God directly brings sin and evil to pass." You do not, however, explain what you mean by evil. As far as one may judge from the example you give in the predetermined act of volition of Adam, you seem to mean by evil the actual exercise of volition, in so far as it is conceived as predetermined in a particular way, or in so far as it is repugnant to the command of God. Hence you conclude (and I agree with you if this be what you mean) that it is absurd to adopt either alternative, either that God brings to pass anything contrary to His own will, or that what is contrary to God's will can be good.

For my own part, I cannot admit that sin and evil have any positive existence, far less that anything can exist, or come to pass, contrary to the will of God. On the contrary, not only do I assert that sin has no positive existence, I also maintain that only in speaking improperly, or humanly, can we say that we sin against God, as in the expression that men offend God.

As to the first point, we know that whatsoever is, when considered in itself without regard to anything else, possesses perfection, extending in each thing as far as the limits of that thing's essence: for essence is nothing else. I take for an illustration the design or determined will of Adam to eat the forbidden fruit. This design or determined will, considered in itself alone, includes perfection in so far as it expresses reality; hence it may be inferred that we can only conceive imperfection in things, when they are viewed in relation to other things possessing more reality: thus in Adam's decision, so long as we view it by itself -and do not compare it with other things more perfect or exhibiting a more perfect state, we can find no imperfection: nay it may be compared with an infinity of other things far less perfect in this respect than itself, such as stones, stocks, &c. This, as a matter of fact, everyone grants. For we all admire in animals qualities which we regard with dislike and aversion in men, such as the pugnacity of bees, the jealousy of doves, &c.; these in human beings are despised, but are nevertheless considered to enhance the value of animals. This being so, it follows that sin, which indicates nothing save imperfection, cannot consistin anything that expresses reality, as we see in the case of Adam's decision and its execution.

Again, we cannot say that Adam's will is at variance with the law of God, and that it is evil because it is displeasing to God; for besides the fact that grave imperfection would be imputed to God, if we say that anything happens contrary to His will, or that He desires anything which He does not obtain, or that His nature resembled that of His creatures in having sympathy with some things more than others; such an occurrence would be at complete variance with the nature of the divine will.

The will of God is identical with His intellect, hence the former can no more be contravened than the latter; in other words, anything which should come to pass against His will must be of a nature to be contrary to His intellect, such, for instance, as a round square. Hence the will or decision of Adam regarded in itself was neither evil nor, properly speaking, against the will of God: it follows that God may—or rather, for the reason you call attention to, must—be its cause; not in so far as it was evil, for the evil in it consisted in the loss of the previous state of being which it entailed on Adam, and it is certain that loss has no positive existence, and is only so spoken of in respect to our and not God's understanding. The difficulty arises from the fact, that we give one and the same definition to all the individuals of a genus, as for instance all who have the outward appearance of men: we accordingly assume all things which are expressed by the same definition to be equally capable of attaining the highest perfection possible for the genus; when we find an individual whose actions are at variance with such perfection, we suppose him to be deprived of it, and to fall short of his nature. We should hardly act in this way, if we did not hark back to the definition and ascribe to the individual a nature in accordance with it. But as God does not know things through abstraction, or form general definitions of the kind above mentioned, and as things have no more reality than the divine understanding and power have put into them and actually endowed them with, it clearly follows that a state of privation can only be spoken of in relation to our intellect, not in relation to God.

Thus, as it seems to me, the difficulty is completely solved. However, in order to make the way still plainer, and remove every doubt, I deem it necessary to answer the two following difficulties:—First, why Holy Scripture says that God wishes for the conversion of the wicked, and also why God forbade Adam to eat of the fruit when He had ordained the contrary? Secondly, that it seems to follow from what I have said, that the wicked by their pride, avarice, and deeds of desperation, worship God in no less degree than the good do by their nobleness, patience, love, &c., inasmuch as both execute God's will.

In answer to the first question, I observe that Scripture, being chiefly fitted for and beneficial to the multitude, speaks popularly after the fashion of men. For the multitude are incapable of grasping sublime conceptions. Hence I am persuaded that all matters, which God revealed to the prophets as necessary to salvation, are set down in the form of laws. With this understanding, the prophets invented whole parables, and represented God as a king and a law-giver, because He had revealed the means of salvation and perdition, and was their cause; the means which were simply causes they styled laws and wrote them down as such; salvation and perdition, which are simply effects necessarily resulting from the aforesaid means, they described as reward and punishment; framing their doctrines more in accordance with such parables than with actual truth. They constantly speak of God as resembling a man, as sometimes angry, sometimes merciful, now desiring what is future, now jealous and suspicious, even as deceived by the devil; so that philosophers and all who are above the law, that is, who follow after virtue, not in obedience to law, but through love, because it is the most excellent of all things, must not be hindered by such expressions.

Thus the command given to Adam consisted solely in this, that God revealed to Adam, that eating of the fruit brought about death; as He reveals to us, through our natural faculties, that poison is deadly. If you ask, for what object did He make this revelation, I answer, in order to render Adam to that extent more perfect in knowledge. Hence, to ask God why He had not bestowed on Adam a more perfect will, is just as absurd as to ask, why the circle has not been endowed with all the properties of a sphere. This follows clearly from what has been said, and I have also proved it in my Principles of Cartesian Philosophy, I. 15.

As to the second difficulty, it is true that the wicked execute after their manner the will of God: but they cannot, therefore, be in any respect compared with the good. The more perfection a thing has, the more does it participate in the deity, and the more does it express perfection. Thus, as the good have incomparably more perfection than the bad, their virtue cannot be likened to the virtue of the wicked, inasmuch as the wicked lack the love of God, which proceeds from the knowledge of God, and by which alone we are, according to our human understanding, called the servants of God. The wicked, knowing not God, are but as instruments in the hand of the workman, serving unconsciously, and perishing in the using; the good, on the other hand, serve consciously, and in serving become more perfect.

1This, Sir, is all I can now contribute to answering your question, and I have no higher wish than that it may satisfy you. But in case you still find any difficulty, I beg you to let me know of that also, to see if I may be able to remove it. You have nothing to fear on your side, but so long as you are not satisfied, I like nothing better than to be informed of your reasons, so that finally the truth may appear. I could have wished to write in the tongue in which I have been brought up. I should, perhaps, have been able to express my thoughts better. But be pleased to take it as it is, amend the mistakes yourself, and believe me,

Your sincere friend and servant.

Long Orchard, near Amsterdam,

Jan. 5, 1665.

LETTER XXXIII.
BLYENBERGH TO SPINOZA.

(A summary only of this letter is here given.—Tr.)

I have two rules in my philosophic inquiries: i. Conformity to reason; ii. Conformity to scripture. I consider the second the most important. Examining your letter by the first, I observe that your identification of God's creative power with His preservative power seems to involve, either that evil does not exist, or else that God brings about evil. If evil be only a term relative to our imperfect knowledge, how do you explain the state of a man who falls from a state of grace into sin? If evil be a negation, how can we have the power to sin? If God causes an evil act, he must cause the evil as well as the act. You say that every man can only act, as he, in fact, does act. This removes all distinction between the good and the wicked. Both, according to you, are perfect. You remove all the sanctions of virtue and reduce us to automata. Your doctrine, that strictly speaking we cannot sin against God, is a hard saying.

[The rest of the letter is taken up with an examination of Spinoza's arguments in respect to their conformity to Scripture.]

Dordrecht, 16 Jan., 1665.

LETTER XXXIV.
SPINOZA TO BLYENBERGH.

[Spinoza complains that Blyenbergh has misunderstood him: he sets forth his true meaning.]

Voorburg, 28 Jan., 1665.

Friend and Sir,—When I read your first letter, I thought that our opinions almost coincided. But from the second, which was delivered to me on the 21st of this month, I see that the matter stands far otherwise, for I perceive that we disagree, not only in remote inferences from first principles, but also in first principles themselves; so that I can hardly think that we can derive any mutual instruction from further correspondence. I see that no proof, though it be by the laws of proof most sound, has any weight with you, unless it agrees with the explanation, which either you yourself, or other theologians known to you, attribute to Holy Scripture. However, if you are convinced that God speaks more clearly and effectually through Holy Scripture than through the natural understanding, which He also has bestowed upon us, and with His divine wisdom keeps continually stable and uncorrupted, you have valid reasons for making your understanding bow before the opinions which you attribute to Holy Scripture; I myself could adopt no different course. For my own part, as I confess plainly, and without circumlocution, that I do not understand the Scriptures, though I have spent some years upon them, and also as I feel that when I have obtained a firm proof, I cannot fall into a state of doubt concerning it, I acquiesce entirely in what is commended to me by my understanding, without any suspicion that I am being deceived in the matter, or that Holy Scripture, though I do not search, could gainsay it: for "truth is not at variance with truth," as I have already clearly shown in my appendix to The Principles of Cartesian Philosophy (I cannot give the precise reference, for I have not the book with me here in the country). But if in any instance I found that a result obtained through my natural understanding was false, I should reckon myself fortunate, for I enjoy life, and try to spend it not in sorrow and sighing, but in peace, joy, and cheerfulness, ascending from time to time a step higher. Meanwhile I know (and this knowledge gives me the highest contentment and peace of mind), that all things come to pass by the power and unchangeable decree of a Being supremely perfect.

To return to your letter, I owe you many and sincere thanks for having confided to me your philosophical opinions; but for the doctrines, which you attribute to me, and seek to infer from my letter, I return you no thanks at all. What ground, I should like to know, has my letter afforded you for ascribing to me the opinions; that men are like beasts, that they die and perish after the manner of beasts, that our actions are displeasing to God, &c.? Perhaps we are most of all at variance on this third point. You think, as far as I can judge, that God takes pleasure in our actions, as though He were a man, who has attained his object, when things fall out as he desired. For my part, have I not said plainly enough, that the good worship God, that in continually serving Him they become more perfect, and that they love God? Is this, I ask, likening them to beasts, or saying that they perish like beasts, or that their actions are displeasing to God? If you had read my letter with more attention, you would have clearly perceived, that our whole dissension lies in the following alternative:—Either the perfections which the good receive are imparted to them by God in His capacity of God, that is absolutely without any human qualities being ascribed to Him—this is what I believe; or else such perfections are imparted by God as a judge, which is what you maintain. For this reason you defend the wicked, saying that they carry out God's decrees as far as in them lies, and therefore serve God no less than the good. But if my doctrine be accepted, this consequence by no means follows; I do not bring in the idea of God as a judge, and, therefore, I estimate an action by its intrinsic merits, not by the powers of its performer; the recompense which follows the action follows from it as necessarily as from the nature of a triangle it follows, that the three angles are equal to two right angles. This may be understood by everyone, who reflects on the fact, that our highest blessedness consists in love towards God, and that such love flows naturally from the knowledge of God, which is so strenuously enjoined on us. The question may very easily be proved in general terms, if we take notice of the nature of God's decrees, as explained in my appendix. However, I confess that all those, who confuse the divine nature with human nature, are gravely hindered from understanding it.

I had intended to end my letter at this point, lest I should prove troublesome to you in these questions, the discussion of which (as I discover from the extremely pious postscript added to your letter) serves you as a pastime and a jest, but for no serious use. However, that I may not summarily deny your request, I will proceed to explain further the words privation and negation, and briefly point out what is necessary for the elucidation of my former letter.

I say then, first, that privation is not the act of depriving, but simply and merely a state of want, which is in itself nothing: it is a mere entity of the reason, a mode of thought framed in comparing one thing with another. We say, for example, that a blind man is deprived of sight, because we readily imagine him as seeing, or else because we compare him with others who can see, or compare his present condition with his past condition when he could see; when we regard the man in this way, comparing his nature either with the nature of others or with his own past nature, we affirm that sight belongs to his nature, and therefore assert that lie has been deprived of it. But when we are considering the nature and decree of God, we cannot affirm privation of sight in the case of the aforesaid man any more than in the case of a stone; for at the actual time sight lies no more within the scope of the man than of the stone; since there belongs to man and forms part of his nature only that which is granted to him by the understanding and will of God. Hence it follows that God is no more the cause of a blind man not seeing, than he is of a stone not seeing. Not seeing is a pure negation. So also, when we consider the case of a man who is led by lustful desires, we compare his present desires with those which exist in the good, or which existed in himself at some other time; we then assert that he is deprived of the better desires, because we conceive that virtuous desires lie within the scope of his nature. This we cannot do, if we consider the nature and decree of God. For, from this point of view, virtuous desires lie at that time no more within the scope of the nature of the lustful man, than within the scope of the nature of the devil or a stone. Hence, from the latter standpoint the virtuous desire is not a privation but a negation.

Thus privation is nothing else than denying of a thing something, which we think belongs to its nature; negation is denying of a thing something, which we do not think belongs to its nature.

We may now see, how Adam's desire for earthly things was evil from our standpoint, but not from God's. Although God knew both the present and the past state of Adam, He did not, therefore, regard Adam as deprived of his past state, that is, He did not regard Adam's past state as within the scope of Adam's present nature. Otherwise God would have apprehended something contrary to His own will, that is, contrary to His own understanding. If you quite grasp my meaning here and at the same time remember, that I do not grant to the mind the same freedom as Descartes does—L[ewis] M[eyer] bears witness to this in his preface to my book—you will perceive, that there is not the smallest contradiction in what I have said. But I see that I should have done far better to have answered you in my first letter with the words of Descartes, to the effect that we cannot know how our freedom and its consequences agree with the foreknowledge and freedom of God (see several passages in my appendix), that, therefore, we can discover no contradiction between creation by God and our freedom, because we cannot understand how God created the universe, nor (what is the same thing) how He preserves it. I thought that you had read the preface, and that by not giving you my real opinions in reply, I should sin against those duties of friendship which I cordially offered you. But this is of no consequence.

Still, as I see that you have not hitherto thoroughly grasped Descartes' meaning, I will call your attention to the two following points. First, that neither Descartes nor I have ever said, that it appertains to our nature to confine the will within the limits of the understanding; we have only said, that God has endowed us with a determined understanding and an undetermined will, so that we know not the object for which He has created us. Further, that an undetermined or perfect will of this kind not only makes us more perfect, but also, as I will presently show you, is extremely necessary for us.

Secondly: that our freedom is not placed in a certain contingency nor in a certain indifference, but in the method of affirmation or denial; so that, in proportion as we are less indifferent in affirmation or denial, so are we more free. For instance, if the nature of God be known to us, it follows as necessarily from our nature to affirm that God exists, as from the nature of a triangle it follows, that the three angles are equal to two right angles; we are never more free, than when we affirm a thing in this way. As this necessity is nothing else but the decree of God (as I have clearly shown in my appendix), we may hence, after a fashion, understand how we act freely and are the cause of our action, though all the time we are acting necessarily and according to the decree of God. This, I repeat, we may, after a fashion, understand, whenever we affirm something, which we clearly and distinctly perceive, but when we assert something which we do not clearly and distinctly understand, in other words, when we allow our will to pass beyond the limits of our understanding, we no longer perceive the necessity nor the decree of God, we can only see our freedom, which is always involved in our will; in which respect only our actions are called good or evil. If we then try to reconcile our freedom with God's decree and continuous creation, we confuse that which we clearly and distinctly understand with that which we do not perceive, and, therefore, our attempt is vain. It is, therefore, sufficient for us to know that we are free, and that we can be so notwithstanding God's decree, and further that we are the cause of evil, because an act can only he called evil in relation to our freedom. I have said thus much for Descartes in order to show that, in the question we are considering, his words exhibit no contradiction.

I will now turn to what concerns myself, and will first briefly call attention to the advantage arising from my opinion, inasmuch as, according to it, our understanding offers our mind and body to God freed from all superstition. Nor do I deny that prayer is extremely useful to us. For my understanding is too small to determine all the means, whereby God leads men to the love of Himself, that is, to salvation. So far is my opinion from being hurtful, that it offers to those, who are not taken up with prejudices and childish superstitions, the only means for arriving at the highest stage of blessedness.

When you say that, by making men so dependent on God, I reduce them to the likeness of the elements, plants or stones, you sufficiently show that you have
thoroughly misunderstood my meaning, and have confused things which regard the understanding with things which regard the imagination. If by your intellect only you had perceived what dependence on God means, you certainly would not think that things, in so far as they depend on God, are dead, corporeal, and imperfect (who ever dared to speak so meanly of the Supremely Perfect Being?); on the contrary, you would understand that for the very reason that they depend on God they are perfect; so that this dependence and necessary operation may best be understood as God's decree, by considering, not stocks and plants, but the most reasonable and perfect creatures. This sufficiently appears from my second observation on the meaning of Descartes, which you ought to have looked to.

I cannot refrain from expressing my extreme astonishment at your remarking, that if God does not punish wrongdoing (that is, as a judge does, with a punishment not intrinsically connected with the offence, for our whole difference lies in this), what reason prevents me from rushing headlong into every kind of wickedness? Assuredly he, who is only kept from vice by the fear of punishment (which I do not think of you), is in no wise acted on by love, and by no means embraces virtue. For my own part, I avoid or endeavour to avoid vice, because it is at direct variance with my proper nature and would lead me astray from the knowledge and love of God.

Again, if you had reflected a little on human nature and the nature of God's decree (as explained in my appendix), and perceived, and known by this time, how a consequence should be deduced from its premises, before a conclusion is arrived at; you would not so rashly have stated that my opinion makes us like stocks, &c.: nor would you have ascribed to me the many absurdities you conjure up.

As to the two points which you say, before passing on to your second rule, that you cannot understand; I answer, that the first may be solved through Descartes, who says that in observing your own nature you feel that you can suspend your judgment. If you say that you do not feel, that you have at present sufficient force to keep your judgment suspended, this would appear to Descartes to be the same as saying that we cannot at present see, that so long as we exist we shall always be thinking things, or retain the nature of thinking things; in fact it would imply a contradiction.

As to your second difficulty, I say with Descartes, that if we cannot extend our will beyond the bounds of our extremely limited understanding, we shall be most wretched—it will not be in our power to eat even a crust of bread, or to walk a step, or to go on living, for all things are uncertain and full of peril.

I now pass on to your second rule, and assert that I believe, though I do not ascribe to Scripture that sort of truth which you think you find in it, I nevertheless assign to it as great if not greater authority than you do. I am far more careful than others not to ascribe to Scripture any childish and absurd doctrines, a precaution which demands either a thorough acquaintance with philosophy or the possession of divine revelations. Hence I pay very little attention to the glosses put upon Scripture by ordinary theologians, especially those of the kind who always interpret Scripture according to the literal and outward meaning: I have never, except among the Socinians, found any theologian stupid enough to ignore that Holy Scripture very often speaks in human fashion of God and expresses its meaning in parables; as for the contradiction which you vainly (in my opinion) endeavour to show, I think you attach to the word parable a meaning different from that usually given. For who ever heard, that a man, who expressed his opinions in parables, had therefore taken leave of his senses? When Micaiah said to King Ahab, that he had seen God sitting on a throne, with the armies of heaven standing on the right hand and the left, and that God asked His angels which of them would deceive Ahab, this was assuredly a parable employed by the prophet on that occasion (which was not fitted for the inculcation of sublime theological doctrines), as sufficiently setting forth the message he had to deliver in the name of God. We cannot say that he had in anywise taken leave of his senses. So also the other prophets of God made manifest God's commands to the people in this fashion as being the best adapted, though not expressly enjoined by God, for leading the people to the primary object of Scripture, which, as Christ Himself says, is to bid men love God above all things, and their neighbour as themselves. Sublime speculations have, in my opinion, no bearing on Scripture. As far as I am concerned I have never learnt or been able to learn any of God's eternal attributes from Holy Scripture.

As to your fifth argument (that the prophets thus made manifest the word of God, since truth is not at variance with truth), it merely amounts, for those who understand the method of proof, to asking me to prove, that Scripture, as it is, is the true revealed word of God. The mathematical proof of this proposition could only be attained by divine revelation. I, therefore, expressed myself as follows: "I believe, but I do not mathematically know, that all things revealed by God to the prophets," &c. Inasmuch as I firmly believe but do not mathematically know, that the prophets were the most trusted counsellors and faithful ambassadors of God. So that in all I have written there is no contradiction, though several such may be found among holders of the opposite opinion.

The rest of your letter (to wit the passage where you say, "Lastly, the supremely perfect Being knew beforehand," &c; and again, your objections to the illustration from poison, and lastly, the whole of what you say of the appendix and what follows) seems to me beside the question.

As regards Lewis Meyer's preface, the points which were still left to be proved by Descartes before establishing his demonstration of free will, are certainly there set forth; it is added that I hold a contrary opinion, my reasons for doing so being given. I shall, perhaps, in due time give further explanations. For the present I have no such intention.

I have never thought about the work on Descartes, nor given any further heed to it, since it has been translated into Dutch. I have my reasons, though it would be tedious to enumerate them here. So nothing remains for me but to subscribe myself, &c.

LETTER XXXV.
BLYENBERGH TO SPINOZA.

[This letter (extending over five pages) is only given here in brief summary.]

The tone of your last letter is very different from that of your first. If our essence is equivalent to our state at a given time, we are as perfect when sinning as when virtuous: God would wish for vice as much as virtue. Both the virtuous and the vicious execute God's will—What is the difference between them? You say some actions are more perfect than others; wherein does this perfection consist? If a mind existed so framed, that vice was in agreement with its proper nature, why should such a mind prefer good to evil? If God makes us all that we are, how can we "go astray"? Can rational substances depend on God in any way except lifelessly? What is the difference between a rational being's dependence on God, and an irrational being's? If we have no free will, are not our actions God's actions, and our will God's will? I could ask several more questions, but do not venture.

P.S. In my hurry I forgot to insert this question: Whether we cannot by foresight avert what would otherwise happen to us?

Dordrecht, 19 Feb., 1665.

LETTER XXXVI.
SPINOZA TO BLYENBERGH.

[Spinoza replies, that there is a difference between the theological and the philosophical way of speaking of God and things divine. He proceeds to discuss Blyenbergh's questions. (Voorburg, 13th March, 1665)]

Friend and Sir,—I have received two letters from you this week; the second, dated 9th March, only served to inform me of the first written on February 19th, and sent to me at Schiedam. In the former I see that you complain of my saying, that "demonstration carried no weight with you," as though I had spoken of my own arguments, which had failed to convince you. Such was far from my intention. I was referring to your own words, which rant as follows:—"And if after long investigation it comes to pass, that my natural knowledge appears either to be at variance with the word (of Scripture), or not sufficiently well, &c.; the word has so great authority with me, that I would rather doubt of the conceptions, which I think I clearly perceive," &c. You see I merely repeat in brief your own phrase, so that I cannot think you have any cause for anger against me, especially as I merely quoted in. order to show the great difference between our standpoints.

Again, as you wrote at the end of your letter that your only hope and wish is to continue in faith and hope, and that all else, which we may become convinced of through our natural faculties, is indifferent to you; I reflected, as I still continue to do, that my letters could be of no use to you, and that I should best consult my own interests by ceasing to neglect my pursuits (which I am compelled while writing to you to interrupt) for the sake of things which could bring no possible benefit. Nor is this contrary to the spirit of my former letter, for in that I looked upon you as simply a philosopher, who (like not a few who call themselves Christians) possesses no touchstone of truth save his natural understanding, and not as a theologian. However, you have taught me to know better, and have also shown me that the foundation, on which I was minded to build up our friendship, has not, as I imagined, been laid.

As for the rest, such are the general accompaniments of controversy, so that I would not on that account transgress the limits of courtesy: I will, therefore, pass over in your second letter, and in this, these and similar expressions, as though they had never been observed. So much for your taking offence; to show you that I have given you no just cause, and, also, that I am quite willing to brook contradiction. I now turn a second time to answering your objections.

I maintain, in the first place, that God is absolutely and really the cause of all things which have essence, whatsoever they may be. If you can demonstrate that evil, error, crime, &c., have any positive existence, which expresses essence, I will fully grant you that God is the cause of crime, evil, error, &c. I believe myself to have sufficiently shown, that that which constitutes the reality of evil, error, crime, &c., does not consist in anything, which expresses essence, and therefore we cannot say that God is its cause. For instance, Nero's matricide, in so far as it comprehended anything positive, was not a crime; the same outward act was perpetrated, and the same matricidal intention was entertained by Orestes; who, nevertheless, is not blamed—at any rate, not so much as Nero. Wherein, then, did Nero's crime consist? In nothing else, but that by his deed he showed himself to be ungrateful, unmerciful, and disobedient. Certainly none of these qualities express aught of essence, therefore God was not the cause of them, though He was the cause of Nero's act and intention.

Further, I would have you observe, that, while we speak philosophically, we ought not to employ theological phrases. For, since theology frequently, and not unwisely, represents God as a perfect man, it is often expedient in theology to say, that God desires a given thing, that He is angry at the actions of the wicked, and delights in those of the good. But in philosophy, when we clearly perceive that the attributes which make men perfect can as ill be ascribed and assigned to God, as the attributes which go to make perfect the elephant and the ass can be ascribed to man; here I say these and similar phrases have no place, nor can we employ them without causing extreme confusion in our conceptions. Hence, in the language of philosophy, it cannot be said that God desires anything of any man, or that anything is displeasing or pleasing to Him: all these are human qualities and have no place in God.

I would have it observed, that although the actions of the good (that is of those who have a clear idea of God, whereby all their actions and their thoughts are determined) and of the wicked (that is of those who do not possess the idea of God, but only the ideas of earthly things, whereby their actions and thoughts are determined), and, in fact, of all things that are, necessarily flow from God's eternal laws and decrees; yet they do not differ from one another in degree only, but also in essence. A mouse no less than an angel, and sorrow no less than joy depend on God; yet a mouse is not a kind of angel, neither is sorrow a kind of joy. I think I have thus answered your objections, if I rightly understand them, for I sometimes doubt, whether the conclusions which you deduce are not foreign to the proposition you are undertaking to prove.

However, this will appear more clearly, if I answer the questions you proposed on these principles. First, Whether murder is as acceptable to God as alms-giving? Secondly, Whether stealing is as good in relation to God as honesty? Thirdly and lastly, Whether if there be a mind so framed, that it would agree with, rather than be repugnant to its proper nature, to give way to lust, and to commit crimes, whether, I repeat, there can be any reason given, why such a mind should do good and eschew evil?

To your first question, I answer, that I do not know, speaking as a philosopher, what you mean by the words "acceptable to God." If you ask, whether God does not hate the wicked, and love the good? whether God does not regard the former with dislike, and the latter with favour? I answer, No. If the meaning of your question is: Are murderers and almsgivers equally good and perfect? my answer is again in the negative. To your second question, I reply: If, by " good in relation to God," you mean that the honest man confers a favour on God, and the thief does Him an injury, I answer that neither the honest man nor the thief can cause God any pleasure or displeasure. If you mean to ask, whether the actions of each, in so far as they possess reality, and are caused by God, are equally perfect? I reply that, if we merely regard the actions and the manner of their execution, both may be equally perfect. If you, therefore, inquire whether the thief and the honest man are equally perfect and blessed? I answer, No. For, by an honest man, I mean one who always desires, that everyone should possess that which is his. This desire, as I prove in my Ethics (as yet unpublished), necessarily derives its origin in the pious from the clear knowledge which they possess, of God and of themselves. As a thief has no desire of the kind, he is necessarily without the knowledge of God and of himself—in other words, without the chief element of our blessedness. If you further ask, What causes you to perform a given action, which I call virtuous, rather than another? I reply, that I cannot know which method, out of the infinite methods at His disposal, God employs to determine you to the said action. It may be, that God has impressed you with a clear idea of Himself, so that you forget the world for love of Him, and love your fellow-men as yourself; it is plain that such a disposition is at variance with those dispositions which are called bad, and, therefore, could not co-exist with them in the same man.

However, this is not the place to expound all the foundations of my Ethics, or to prove all that I have advanced; I am now only concerned in answering your questions, and defending myself against them.

Lastly, as to your third question, it assumes a contradiction, and seems to me to be, as though one asked: If it agreed better with a man's nature that he should hang himself, could any reasons be given for his not hanging himself? Can such a nature possibly exist? If so, I maintain (whether I do or do not grant free will), that such an one, if he sees that he can live more conveniently on the gallows than sitting at his own table, would act most foolishly, if he did not hang himself. So anyone who clearly saw that, by committing crimes, he would enjoy a really more perfect and better life and existence, than he could attain by the practice of virtue, would be foolish if he did not act on his convictions. For, with such a perverse human nature as his, crime would become virtue.

As to the other question, which you add in your postscript, seeing that one might ask a hundred such in an hour, without arriving at a conclusion about any, and seeing that you yourself do not press for an answer, I will send none.

I will now only subscribe myself, &c.

LETTER XXXVII.
BLYENBERGH TO SPINOZA.

[Blyenbergh, who had been to see Spinoza, asks the latter to send him a report of their conversation, and to answer five fresh questions. (Dordrecht, 27th March, 1665)]

Omitted.

LETTER XXXVIII.
SPINOZA TO BLYENBERGH.

[Spinoza declines further correspondence with Blyenbergh, but says he will give explanations of certain points by word of mouth. (Voorburg, 3rd June, 1665)] 1

Friend and Sir,—When your letter, dated 27th March, was delivered to me, I was just starting for Amsterdam. I, therefore, after reading half of it, left it at home, to be answered on my return: for I thought it dealt only with questions raised in our first controversy. However, a second perusal showed me, that it embraced a far wider subject, and not only asked me for a proof of what, in my preface to "Principles of Cartesian Philosophy," I wrote (with the object of merely stating, without proving or urging my opinion), but also requested me to impart a great portion of my Ethics, which, as everyone knows, ought to be based on physics and metaphysics. For this reason, I have been unable to allow myself to satisfy your demands. I wished to await an opportunity for begging you, in a most friendly way, by word of mouth, to withdraw your request, for giving you my reasons for refusal, and for showing that your inquiries do not promote the solution of our first controversy, but, on the contrary, are for the most part entirely dependent on its previous settlement. So far are they not essential to the understanding of my doctrine concerning necessity, that they cannot be apprehended, unless the latter question is understood first. However, before such an opportunity offered, a second letter reached me this week, appearing to convey a certain sense of displeasure at my delay. Necessity, therefore, has compelled me to write you these few words, to acquaint you more fully with my proposal and decision. I hope that, when the facts of the case are before you, you will, of your own accord, desist from your request, and will still remain kindly disposed towards me. I, for my part, will, in all things, according to my power, prove myself your, &c.

XXXIX.
SPINOZA TO CHRISTIAN HUYGHENS.

(Treating of the Unity of God.)

Distinguished Sir,—The demonstration of the unity of God, on the ground that His nature involves necessary existence, which you asked for, and I took note of, I have been prevented by various business from sending to you before. In order to accomplish my purpose, I will premise—

I. That the true definition of anything includes nothing except the simple nature of the thing defined. From this it follows

II. That no definition can involve or express a multitude or a given number of individuals, inasmuch as it involves and expresses nothing except the nature of the thing as it is in itself. For instance, the definition of a triangle includes nothing beyond the simple nature of a triangle; it does not include any given number of triangles. In like manner, the definition of the mind as a thinking thing, or the definition of God as a perfect Being, includes nothing beyond the natures of the mind and of God, not a given number of minds or gods.

III. That for everything that exists there must necessarily be a positive cause, through which it exists.

IV. This cause may be situate either in the nature and definition of the thing itself (to wit, because existence belongs to its nature or necessarily includes it), or externally to the thing.

From these premises it follows, that if any given number of individuals exists in nature, there must be one or more causes, which have been able to produce exactly that number of individuals, neither more nor less. If, for instance, there existed in nature twenty men (in order to avoid all confusion, I will assume that these all exist together as primary entities), it is not enough to investigate the cause of human nature in general, in order to account for the existence of these twenty; we must also inquire into the reason, why there exist exactly twenty men, neither more nor less. For (by our third hypothesis) for each man a reason and a cause must be forthcoming, why he should exist. But this cause (by our second and third hypotheses) cannot be contained in the nature of man himself; for the true definition of man does not involve the number of twenty men. Hence (by our fourth hypothesis) the cause for the existence of these twenty men, and consequently for the existence of each of them, must exist externally to them. We may thus absolutely conclude, that all things, which are conceived to exist in the plural number, must necessarily be produced by external causes and not by the force of their own nature. But since (by our second hypothesis) necessary existence appertains to the nature of God, His true definition must necessarily include necessary existence: therefore from His true definition His necessary existence must be inferred. But from His true definition (as I have already demonstrated from our second and third hypotheses) the necessary existence of many gods cannot be inferred. Therefore there only follows the existence of a single God. Which was to be proved.

This, distinguished Sir, has now seemed to me the best method for demonstrating the proposition. I have also proved it differently by means of the distinction between essence and existence; but bearing in mind the object you mentioned to me, I have preferred to send you the demonstration given above. I hope it will satisfy you, and I will await your reply, meanwhile remaining, &c.

Voorburg, 7 Jan., 1666.

LETTER XL.
SPINOZA TO CHRISTIAN HUYGHENS.

Further arguments for the unity of God.

Distinguished Sir,—In your last letter, written on March 30th, you have excellently elucidated the point, which was somewhat obscure to me in your letter of February 10th. As I now know your opinion, I will set forth the state of the question as you conceive it; whether there be only a single Being who subsists by his own sufficiency or force? I not only affirm this to be so, but also undertake to prove it from the fact, that the nature of such a Being necessarily involves existence; perhaps it may also be readily proved from the understanding of God (as I set forth, "Principles of Cartesian Philosophy," I. Prop. i.), or from others of His attributes. Before treating of the subject I will briefly show, as preliminaries, what properties must be possessed by a Being including necessary existence. To wit:—

I. It must be eternal. For if a definite duration be assigned to it, it would beyond that definite duration be conceived as non-existent, or as not involving necessary existence, which would be contrary to its definition.

II. It must be simple, not made up of parts. For parts must in nature and knowledge be prior to the whole they compose: this could not be the case with regard to that which is eternal.

III. It cannot be conceived as determinate, but only as infinite. For, if the nature of the said Being were determinate, and conceived as determinate, that nature would beyond the said limits be conceived as non-existent, which again is contrary to its definition.

IV. It is indivisible. For if it were divisible, it could be divided into parts, either of the same or of different nature. If the latter, it could be destroyed and so not exist, which is contrary to its definition; if the former, each part would in itself include necessary existence, and thus one part could exist without others, and consequently be conceived as so existing. Hence the nature of the Being would be comprehended as finite, which, by what has been said, is contrary to its definition. Thus we see that, in attempting to ascribe to such a Being any imperfection, we straightway fall into contradictions. For, whether the imperfection which we wish to assign to the said Being be situate in any defect, or in limitations possessed by its nature, or in any change which it might, through deficiency of power, undergo from external causes, we are always brought back to the contradiction, that a nature which involves necessary existence, does not exist, or does not necessarily exist. I conclude, therefore—

V. That everything, which includes necessary existence, cannot have in itself any imperfection, but must express pure perfection.

VI. Further, since only from perfection can it come about, that any Being should exist by its own sufficiency and force, it follows that, if we assume a

Being to exist by its own nature, but not to express all perfections, we must further suppose that another Being exists, which does comprehend in itself all perfections. For, if the less powerful Being exists by its own sufficiency, how much more must the more powerful so exist?

Lastly, to deal with the question, I affirm that there can only be a single Being, of which the existence belongs to its nature; such a Being which possesses in itself all perfections I will call God. If there be any Being to whose nature existence belongs, such a Being can contain in itself no imperfection, but must (by my fifth premiss) express every perfection; therefore, the nature of such a Being seems to belong to God (whose existence we are bound to affirm by Premiss VI.), inasmuch as He has in Himself all perfections and no imperfections. Nor can it exist externally to God. For if, externally to God, there existed one and the same nature involving necessary existence, such nature would be twofold; but this, by what we have just shown, is absurd. Therefore there is nothing save God, but there is a single God, that involves necessary existence, which was to be proved.

Such, distinguished Sir, are the arguments I can now produce for demonstrating this question. I hope I may also demonstrate to you, that I am, &c.

Voorburg, 10 April, 1666.

LETTER XLI.
SPINOZA TO CHRISTIAN HUYGHENS.

[Further discussion concerning the unity of God. Spinoza asks for advice about polishing lenses. (Voorburg, May, 1666.)]

Distinguished Sir,—I have been by one means or another prevented from answering sooner your letter, dated 19th May. As I gather that you suspend your judgment with regard to most of the demonstration I sent you (owing, I believe, to the obscurity you find in it), I will here endeavour to explain its meaning more clearly.

First I enumerated four properties, which a Being existing by its own sufficiency or force must possess. These four, and others like them, I reduced in my fifth observation to one. Further, in order to deduce all things necessary for the demonstration from a single premiss, I endeavoured in my sixth observation to demonstrate the existence of God from the given hypothesis; whence, lastly, taking (as you know) nothing beyond the ordinary meaning of the terms, I drew the desired conclusion.

Such, in brief, was my purpose and such my aim. I will now explain the meaning of each step singly, and will first start with the aforesaid four properties.

In the first you find no difficulty, nor is it anything but, as in the case of the second, an axiom. By simple I merely mean not compound, or not made up of parts differing in nature or other parts agreeing in nature. This demonstration is assuredly universal.

The sense of my third observation (that if the Being be thought, it cannot be conceived as limited by thought, but only as infinite, and similarly, if it be extension, it cannot be conceived as limited by extension) you have excellently perceived, though you say you do not perceive the conclusion; this last is based on the fact, that a contradiction is involved in conceiving under the category of non-existence anything, whose definition includes or (what is the same thing) affirms existence. And since determination implies nothing positive, but only a limitation of the existence of the nature conceived as determinate, it follows that that, of which the definition affirms existence, cannot be conceived as determinate. For instance, if the term extension included necessary existence, it would be alike impossible to conceive extension without existence and existence without extension. If this were established, it would be impossible to conceive determinate extension. For, if it be conceived as determinate, it must be determined by its own nature, that is by extension, and this extension, whereby it is determined, must be conceived under the category of non-existence, which by the hypothesis is obviously a contradiction. In my fourth observation, I merely wished to show, that such a Being could neither be divided into parts of the same nature or parts of a different nature, whether those of a different nature involved necessary existence or not. If, I said, we adopt the second view, the Being would be destroyed; for destruction is merely the resolution of a thing into parts so that none of them expresses the nature of the whole; if we adopt the first view, we should be in contradiction with the first three properties.

In my fifth observation, I merely asserted, that perfection consists in being, and imperfection in the privation of being. I say the privation; for although extension denies of itself thought, this argues no imperfection in it. It would be an imperfection in it, if it were in any degree deprived of extension, as it would be, if it were determinate; or again, if it lacked duration, position, &c.

My sixth observation you accept absolutely, and yet you say, that your whole difficulty remains (inasmuch as there may be, you think, several self-existent entities of different nature; as for instance thought and extension are different and perhaps subsist by their own sufficiency). I am, therefore, forced to believe, that you attribute to my observation a meaning quite different from the one intended by me. I think I can discern your interpretation of it; however, in order to save time, I will merely set forth my own meaning. I say then, as regards my sixth observation, that if we assert that anything, which is indeterminate and perfect only after its kind, exists by its own sufficiency, we must also grant the existence of a Being indeterminate and perfect absolutely; such a Being I will call God. If, for example, we wish to assert that extension or thought (which are each perfect after their kind, that is, in a given sphere of being) exists by its own sufficiency, we must grant also the existence of God, who is absolutely perfect, that is of a Being absolutely indeterminate. I would here direct attention to what I have just said with regard to the term imperfection; namely, that it signifies that a thing is deficient in some quality, which, nevertheless, belongs to its nature. For instance, extension can only be called imperfect in respect of duration, position, or quantity: that is, as not enduring longer, as not retaining its position, or as not being greater. It can never be called imperfect, because it does not think, inasmuch as its nature requires nothing of the kind, but consists solely in extension, that is in a certain sphere of being. Only in respect to its own sphere can it be called determinate or indeterminate, perfect or imperfect. Now, since the nature of God is not confined to a certain sphere of being, but exists in being, which is absolutely indeterminate, so His nature also demands everything which perfectly expresses being; otherwise His nature would be determinate and deficient.

This being so, it follows that there can be only one Being, namely God, who exists by His own force. If, for the sake of an illustration, we assert, that extension involves existence; it is, therefore, necessary that it should be eternal and indeterminate, and express absolutely no imperfection, but perfection. Hence extension will appertain to God, or will be something which in some fashion expresses the nature of God, since God is a Being, who not only in a certain respect but absolutely is in essence indeterminate and omnipotent. What we have here said oy way of illustration regarding extension must be asserted of all that we ascribe a similar existence to. I, therefore, conclude as in my former letter, that there is nothing external to God, but that God alone exists by His own sufficiency. I think I have said enough to show the meaning of my former letter; however, of this you will be the best judge. * * * * *

(The rest of the letter is occupied with details about the polishing of lenses.)

LETTER XLI.A.
SPINOZA TO ANON. 1 (May or June, 1665).

[Spinoza urges his correspondent to be diligent in studying philosophy, promises to send part of the Ethics, and adds some personal details.]

Dear Friend,—I do not know whether you have quite forgotten me; but there are many circumstances which lead me to suspect it. First, when I was setting out on. my journey, 2 I wished to bid you good-bye; and, after your own invitation, thinking I should certainly find you at home, heard that you had gone to the Hague. I return to Voorburg, nothing doubting but that you would at least have visited me in passing; but you, forsooth, without greeting your friend, went back home. Three weeks have I waited, without getting sight of a letter from you. If you wish this opinion of mine to be changed, you may easily change it by writing; and you can, at the sametime, point out a means of entering into a correspondence, as we once talked of doing at your house.

Meanwhile, I should like to ask you, nay I do beg and entreat you, by our friendship, to apply yourself to some serious work with real study, and to devote the chief part of your life to the cultivation of your understanding and your soul. Now, while there is time, and before you complain of having let time and, indeed, your own self slip by. Further, in order to set our correspondence on foot, and to give you courage to write to me more freely, I would have you know that I have long thought, and, indeed, been almost certain, that you are somewhat too diffident of your own abilities, and that you are afraid of advancing some question or proposal unworthy of a man of learning. It does not become me to praise you, and expatiate on your talents to your face; but, if you are afraid that I shall show your letters to others, who will laugh at you, I give you my word of honour, that I will religiously keep them, and will show them to no mortal without your leave. On these conditions, you may enter on a correspondence, unless you doubt of my good faith, which I do not in the least believe. I want to hear your opinion on this in your first letter; and you may, at the same time, send me the conserve of red roses, though I am now much better.

After my journey, I was once bled; but the fever did not cease, though I was somewhat more active than before the bleeding, owing, I think, to the change of air; but I was two or three times laid up with a tertian. This, however, by good diet, I have at length driven away, and sent about its business. Where it has gone, I know not; but I am taking care it does not return here.

As regards the third part of my philosophy, I will shortly send it you, if you wish to be its transmitter, or to our friend De Vries; and, although I had settled not to send any of it, till it was finished, yet, as it takes longer than I thought, I am unwilling to keep you waiting. I will send up to the eightieth proposition, or thereabouts.

Of English affairs I hear a good deal, but nothing for certain. The people continue to be apprehensive, and can see no reason, why the fleet should not be despatched; but the matter does not yet seem to be set on foot. I am afraid our rulers want to be overwise and prudent; but the event will show what they intend, and what they will attempt. May the gods turn it all to good. I want to know, what our people think, where you are, and what they know for certain; but, above all things, I want you to believe me, &c.

LETTER XLII.
SPINOZA TO I. B. 1

[Concerning the best method, by which we may safely arrive at the knowledge of things.]

Most learned Sir and Dearest Friend,—I have not been able hitherto to answer your last letter, received some time back. I have been so hindered by various occupations and calls on my time, that I am hardly yet free from them. However, as I have a few spare moments, I do not want to fall short of my duty, but take this first opportunity of heartily thanking you for your affection and kindness towards me, which you have often displayed in your actions, and now also abundantly prove by your letter.

I pass on to your question, which runs as follows: "Is there, or can there be, any method by which we may, without hindrance, arrive at the knowledge of the most excellent things? or are our minds, like our bodies, subject to the vicissitudes of circumstance, so that our thoughts are governed rather by fortune than by skill?" I think I shall satisfy you, if I show that there must necessarily be a method, whereby we are able to direct our clear and distinct perceptions, and that our mind is not, like our body, subject to the vicissitudes of circumstance.

This conclusion may be based simply on the consideration that one clear and distinct perception, or several such together, can be absolutely the cause of another clear and distinct perception. Now, all the clear and distinct perceptions, which we form, can only arise from other clear and distinct perceptions, which are in us; nor do they acknowledge any cause external to us. Hence it follows that the clear and distinct perceptions, which we form, depend solely on our nature, and on its certain and fixed laws; in other words, on our absolute power, not on fortune—that is, not on causes which, although also acting by certain and fixed laws, are yet unknown to us, and alien to our nature and power. As regards other perceptions, I confess that they depend chiefly on fortune. Hence clearly appears, what the true method ought to be like, and what it ought chiefly to consist in—namely, solely in the knowledge of the pure understanding, and its nature and laws. In order that such knowledge may be acquired, it is before all things necessary to distinguish between the understanding and the imagination, or between ideas which are true and the rest, such as the fictitious, the false, the doubtful, and absolutely all which depend solely on the memory. For the understanding of these matters, as far as the method requires, there is no need to know the nature of the mind through its first cause; it is sufficient to put together a short history of the mind, or of perceptions, in the manner taught by Verulam.

I think that in these few words I have explained and demonstrated the true method, and have, at the same time, pointed out the way of acquiring it. It only remains to remind you, that all these questions demand assiduous study, and great firmness of disposition and purpose. In order to fulfil these conditions, it is of prime necessity to follow a fixed mode and plan of living, and to set before one some definite aim. But enough of this for the present, &c.

    Voorburg, 10 June, 1666.

LETTER XLIII.
SPINOZA TO I. v. M. 1

[Spinoza solves for his friend an arithmetical problem connected with games of chance. (Voorburg, Oct. 1, 1666.)]

Omitted.

LETTERS XLIV., XLV., XLVI. (XXXIX., XL., XLI.) SPINOZA TO I. I. 2

XLIV. [Remarks on Descartes' treatise on Optics.]

XLV. [Remarks on some alchemistic experiments, on the third and fourth meditations of Descartes, and on Optics.]

XLVI. [Remarks on Hydrostatics.]

LETTER XLVII.
SPINOZA TO I. I.

[Spinoza begs his friend to stop the printing of the Dutch version of the Tractatus Theologico-Politicus. Some remarks on a pernicious pamphlet, "Homo Politicus," and on Thales of Miletus.]

Most courteous Sir,—When Professor N. N. visited me the other day, he told me that my Theologico-Political Treatise has been translated into Dutch, and that someone, whose name he did not know, was about printing it. With regard to this, I earnestly beg you to inquire carefully into the business, and, if possible, stop the printing. This is the request not only of myself, but of many of my friends and acquaintances, who would be sorry to see the book placed under an interdict, as it undoubtedly would be, if published in Dutch. I do not doubt, but that you will do this service to me and the cause.

One of my friends sent me a short time since a pamphlet called "Homo Politicus," of which I had heard much. I have read it, and find it to be the most pernicious work which men could devise or invent. Rank and riches are the author's highest good; he adapts his doctrine accordingly, and shows the means to acquire them; to wit, by inwardly rejecting all religion, and outwardly professing whatever best serves his own advancement, also by keeping faith with no one, except in so far as he himself is profited thereby. For the rest, to feign, to make promises and break them,, to lie, to swear falsely, and many such like practices call forth his highest praises. When I had finished reading the book, I debated whether I should write a pamphlet indirectly aimed against its author, wherein I should treat of the highest good and show the troubled and wretched condition of those who are covetous of rank and riches; finally proving by very plain reasoning and many examples, that the insatiable desire for rank and riches must bring and has brought ruin to states.

How much better and more excellent than the doctrines of the aforesaid writer are the reflections of Thales of Miletus, appears from the following. All the goods of friends, he says, are in common; wise men are the friends of the gods, and all things belong to the gods; therefore all things belong to the wise. Thus in a single sentence, this wisest of men accounts himself most rich, rather by nobly despising riches than by sordidly seeking them. In other passages he shows that the wise lack riches, not from necessity, but from choice. For when his friends reproached him with his poverty he answered, "Do you wish me to show you, that I could acquire what I deem unworthy of my labour, but you so diligently seek?" On their answering in the affirmative, he hired every oil-press in the whole of Greece (for being a distinguished astrologer he knew that the olive harvest would be as abundant as in previous years it had been scanty), and sub-let at his own price what he had hired for a very small sum, thus acquiring in a single year a large fortune, which he bestowed liberally as he had gained it industriously, &c.

The Hague, 17 Feb., 1671.

LETTER XLVIII.

Written by a physician, Lambert de Velthuysen, to Isaac Orobio, and forwarded by the latter to Spinoza. It contains a detailed attack on the Tractatus Theologico-Politicus. Its tenor may be sufficiently seen from Spinoza's reply. (Written at Utrecht, January 24th, 1671.) Velthuysen afterwards became more friendly to Spinoza, as appears from Letter LXXV.

LETTER XLIX.
SPINOZA TO ISAAC OROBIO. 1

[A defence of the Tractatus Theologico-Politicus. (The Hague, 1671.)]

Most learned Sir,—You doubtless wonder why I have kept you so long waiting. I could hardly bring myself to reply to the pamphlet of that person, which you thought fit to send me; indeed I only do so now because of my promise. However, in order as far as possible to humour my feelings, I will fulfil my engagement in as few words as I can, and will briefly show how perversely he has interpreted my meaning; whether through malice or through ignorance I cannot readily say. But to the matter in hand.

First he says, "that it is of little moment to know what nation I belong to, or what sort of life I lead." Truly, if he had known, he would not so easily have persuaded himself that I teach Atheism. For Atheists are wont greedily to covet rank and riches, which I have always despised, as all who know me are aware. Again, in order to smooth his path to the object he has in view, he says that, "I am possessed of no mean talents," so that he may, forsooth, more easily convince his readers, that I have knowingly and cunningly with evil intent argued for the cause of the deists, in order to discredit it. This contention sufficiently shows that he has not understood my reasons. For who could be so cunning and clever, as to be able to advance under false pretences so many and such good reasons for a doctrine which he did not believe in? Who will pass for an honest writer in the eyes of a man, that thinks one may argue as soundly for fiction as for truth? But after all I am not astonished. Descartes was formerly served in the same way by Voët, and the most honourable writers are constantly thus treated.

He goes on to say, "In order to shun the reproach of superstition, he seems to me to have thrown off all religion." What this writer means by religion and what by superstition, I know not. But I would ask, whether a man throws off all religion, who maintains that God must be acknowledged as the highest good, and must, as such, be loved with a free mind? or, again, that the reward of virtue is virtue itself, while the punishment of folly and weakness is folly itself? or, lastly, that every man ought to love his neighbour, and to obey the commands of the supreme power? Such doctrines I have not only expressly stated, but have also demonstrated them by very solid reasoning. However, I think I see the mud wherein this person sticks. He finds nothing in virtue and the understanding in themselves to please him, but would prefer to live in accordance with his passions, if it were not for the single obstacle that he fears punishment. He abstains from evil actions, and obeys the divine commands like a slave, with unwillingness and hesitation, expecting as the reward of his bondage to be recompensed by God with gifts far more pleasing than divine love, and greater in proportion to his dislike to goodness and consequent unwillingness to practise it. Hence it comes to pass, that he believes that all, who are not restrained by this fear, lead a life of licence and throw off all religion. But this I pass over, and proceed to the deduction, whereby he wishes to show, that "with covert and disguised arguments I teach atheism." The foundation of his reasoning is, that he thinks I take away freedom from God, and subject Him to fate. This is flatly false. For I have maintained, that all things follow by inevitable necessity from the nature of God, in the same way as all maintain that it follows from the nature of God, that He understands Himself: no one denies that this latter consequence follows necessarily from the divine nature, yet no one conceives that God is constrained by any fate; they believe that He understands Himself with entire freedom, though necessarily. I find nothing here, that cannot be perceived by everyone; if, nevertheless, my adversary thinks that these arguments are advanced with evil intent, what does he think of his own Descartes, who asserted that nothing is done by us, which has not been pre-ordained by God, nay, that we are newly created as it were by God every moment, though none the less we act according to our own free will? This, as Descartes himself confesses, no one can understand.

Further, this inevitable necessity in things destroys neither divine laws nor human. For moral principles, whether they have received from God the form of laws or not, are nevertheless divine and salutary. Whether we accept the good, which follows from virtue and the divine love, as given us by God as a judge, or as emanating from the necessity of the divine nature, it is not in either case more or less to be desired; nor are the evils which follow from evil actions less to be feared, because they follow necessarily: finally, whether we act under necessity or freedom, we are in either case led by hope and fear. Wherefore the assertion is false, "that I maintain that there is no room left for precepts and commands." Or as he goes on to say, "that there is no expectation of reward or punishment, since all things are ascribed to fate, and are said to flow with inevitable necessity from God."

I do not here inquire, why it is the same, or almost the same to say that all things necessarily flow from God, as to say that God is universal; but I would have you observe the insinuation which he not less maliciously subjoins, "that I wish that men should practise virtue, not because of the precepts and law of God, or through hope of reward and fear of punishment, but," &c. Such a sentiment you will assuredly not find anywhere in my treatise: on the contrary, I have expressly stated in Chap. IV., that the sum of the divine law (which, as I have said in Chap. II., has been divinely inscribed on our hearts), and its chief precept is, to love God as the highest good: not, indeed, from the fear of any punishment, for love cannot spring from fear; nor for the love of anything which we desire for our own delight, for then we should love not God, but the object of our desire.

Î have shown in the same chapter, that God revealed this law to the prophets, so that, whether it received from God the form of a command, or whether we conceive it to be like God's other decrees, which involve eternal necessity and truth, it will in either case remain God's decree and a salutary principle. Whether I love God in freedom, or whether I love Him from the necessity of the divine decree, I shall nevertheless love God, and shall be in a state of salvation. Wherefore, I can now declare here, that this person is one of that sort, of whom I have said at the end of my preface, that I would rather that they utterly neglected my book, than that by misinterpreting it after their wont, they should become hostile, and hinder others without benefiting themselves.

Though I think I have said enough to prove what I intended, I have yet thought it worth while to add a few observations—namely, that this person falsely thinks, that I have in view the axiom of theologians, which draws a distinction between the words of a prophet when propounding doctrine, and the same prophet when narrating an event. If by such an axiom he means that which in Chap. XV. I attributed to a certain R. Jehuda Alpakhar, how could he think that I agree with it, when in that very chapter I reject it as false? If he does not mean this, I confess I am as yet in ignorance as to what he does mean, and, therefore, could not have had it in view.

Again, I cannot see why he says, that all will adopt my opinions, who deny that reason and philosophy should be the interpreters of Scripture; I have refuted the doctrine of such persons, together with that of Maimonides.

It would take too long to review all the indications he gives of not having judged me altogether calmly. I therefore pass on to his conclusion, where he says, "that I have no arguments left to prove, that Mahomet was not a true prophet." This he endeavours to show from my opinions, whereas from them it clearly follows, that Mahomet was an impostor, inasmuch as he utterly forbids that freedom, which the Catholic religion revealed by our natural faculties and by the prophets grants, and which I have shown should be granted in its completeness. Even if this were not so, am I, I should like to know, bound to show that any prophet is false? Surely the burden lies with the prophets, to prove that they are true. But if he retorts, that Mahomet also taught the divine law, and gave certain signs of his mission, as the rest of the prophets did, there is surely no reason why he should deny, that Mahomet also was a true prophet.

As regards the Turks and other non-Christian nations;, if they worship God by the practice of justice and charity towards their neighbour, I believe that they have the spirit of Christ, and are in a state of salvation, whatever they may ignorantly hold with regard to Mahomet and oracles.

Thus you see, my friend, how far this man has strayed from the truth; nevertheless, I grant that he has inflicted the greatest injury, not on me but on himself, inasmuch as he has not been ashamed to declare, that "under disguised and covert arguments I teach atheism."

I do not think, that you will find any expressions I have used against this man too .severe. However, if there be any of the kind which offend you, I beg you to correct them, as you shall think fit. I have no disposition to irritate him, whoever he may be, and to raise up by my labours, enemies against myself; as this is often the result of disputes like the present, I could scarcely prevail on myself to reply—nor should I have prevailed, if I had not promised. Farewell. I commit to your prudence this letter, and myself, who am, &c.

LETTER L.
SPINOZA TO JARIG JELLIS.

[Of the difference between the political theories of Hobbes and Spinoza, of the Unity of God, of the notion of figure, of the book of a Utrecht professor against the Tractatus Theologico-Politicus.]

Most courteous Sir,—As regards political theories, the difference which you inquire about between Hobbes and myself, consists in this, that I always preserve natural right intact, and only allot to the chief magistrates in every state a right over their subjects commensurate with the excess of their power over the power of the subjects. This is what always takes place in the state of nature.

Again, with regard to the demonstration which I establish in the appendix to my geometric exposition of Cartesian principles, namely, that God can only with great impropriety be called one or single, I answer that a thing can only be called one or single in respect of existence, not in respect of essence. For we do not conceive things under the category of numbers, unless they have first been reduced to a common genus. For example, he who holds in his hand a penny and a crown piece will not think of the twofold number, unless he can call both the penny and the crown piece by one and the same name, to wit, coins or pieces of money. In the latter case he can say that he holds two coins or pieces of money, inasmuch as he calls the crown as well as the penny, a coin, or piece of money. Hence, it is evident that a thing cannot be called one or single, unless there be afterwards another thing conceived, which (as has been said) agrees with it. Now, since the existence of God is His essence, and of His essence we can form no general idea, it is certain, that he who calls God one or single has no true idea of God, and speaks of Him very improperly.

As to the doctrine that figure is negation and not anything positive, it is plain that the whole of matter considered indefinitely can have no figure, and that figure can only exist in finite and determinate bodies. For he who says, that he perceives a figure, merely indicates thereby, that he conceives a determinate thing, and how it is determinate. This determination, therefore, does not appertain to the thing according to its being, but, on the contrary, is its non-being. As then figure is nothing else than determination, and determination is negation, figure, as has been said, can be nothing but negation.

The book, which a Utrecht professor wrote against mine, and which was published after his death, I saw lying in a bookseller's window. From the little I then read of it, I judged it unworthy of perusal, still less of reply. I, therefore, left the book, and its author. With an inward smile I reflected, that the most ignorant are ever the most audacious and the most ready to rush into print. The Christians seem to me to expose their wares for sale like hucksters, who always show first that which is worst. The devil is said to be very cunning, but to my thinking the tricks of these people are in cunning far beyond his. Farewell.

The Hague, 2 June, 1674.

LETTER LI.
GODFREY LEIBNITZ TO SPINOZA.

Distinguished Sir,—Among your other merits spread abroad by fame, I understand that you have remarkable skill in optics. I have, therefore, wished to forward my essay, such as it is, to you, as I am not likely to find a better critic in this branch of learning. The paper, which I send you, and which I have styled "a note on advanced optics," has been published with the view of more conveniently making known my ideas to my friends and the curious in such matters. I hear that * * * * * is very clever in the same subject, doubtless he is well known to you. 1 If you could obtain for me his opinion and kind attention, you would greatly increase my obligation to you. The paper explains itself.

I believe you have already received the "Prodromo" of Francis Lana 1 the Jesuit, written in Italian. Some remarkable observations on optics are contained in it. John Oltius too, a young Swiss very learned in these matters, has published "Physico-Mechanical Reflections concerning Vision;" in which he announces a machine for the polishing all kinds of glasses, very simple and of universal applicability, and also declares that he has discovered a means of collecting all the rays coming from different points of an object, so as to obtain an equal number of corresponding points, but only under conditions of a given distance and form of object. My proposal is, not that the rays from all points should be collected and re-arranged (this is with any object of distance impossible at the present stage of our knowledge); the result I aim at is the equal collection of rays from points outside the optic axis and in the optic axis, so that the apertures of glasses could be made of any size desired without impairing the distinctness of vision. But this must stand according to your skilled verdict. Farewell, and believe me, distinguished Sir, your obedient servant,

Godfrey Leibnitz,
J. U. D., Councillor of the Elector of Mainz.
Frankfort, 5 Oct., 1671 (new style).

LETTER LII.
SPINOZA TO LEIBNITZ.

[Answer to the foregoing letter].

Most learned and distinguished Sir,—I have read the paper you were kind enough to send me, and return you many thanks for the communication. I regret that I have not been able quite to follow your meaning, though you explain it sufficiently clearly, whether you think that there is any cause for making the apertures of the glasses small, except that the rays coming from a single point are not collected accurately at another single point, but in a small area which we generally call the mechanical point, and that this small area is greater or less in proportion to the size of the aperture. Further, I ask whether the lenses which you call "pandochæ" correct this fault, so that the mechanical point or small area, on which the rays coming from a single point are after refraction collected, always preserves the same proportional size, whether the aperture be small or large. If so, one may enlarge the aperture as much as one likes, and consequently these lenses will be far superior to those of any other shape known to me; if not, I hardly see why you praise them so greatly beyond common lenses. For circular lenses have everywhere the same axis; therefore, when we employ them, we must regard all the points of an object as placed in the optic axis; although all the points of the object be not at the same distance, the difference arising thence will not be perceptible, when the objects are very remote; because then the rays coming from a single point would, as they enter the glass, be regarded as parallel. I think your lenses might be of service in obtaining a more distinct representation of all the objects, when we wish to include several objects in one view, as we do, when we employ very large convex circular lenses. However, I would rather suspend my judgment about all these details, till you have more clearly explained your meaning, as I heartily beg you to do. I have, as you requested, sent the other copy of your paper to Mr. * * * *. He answers, that he has at present no time to study it, but he hopes to have leisure in a week or two.

I have not yet seen the "Prodromo" of Francis Lana, nor the "Physico-Mechanical Reflections" of John Oltius. What I more regret is, that your "Physical Hypothesis" has not yet come to my hands, nor is there a copy for sale here at the Hague. The gift, therefore, which you so liberally promise me will be most acceptable to me; if I can be of use to you in any other matter, you will always find me most ready. I hope you will not think it too irksome to reply to this short note.

Distinguished Sir,
Yours sincerely,
B. DE SPINOZA.
The Hague, 9 Nov., 1671.

P.S. Mr. Diemerbroech does not live here. I am, therefore, forced to entrust this to an ordinary letter-carrier. I doubt not that you know someone at the Hague, who would take charge of our letters; I should like to hear of such a person, that our correspondence might be more conveniently and securely taken care of. If the "Tractatus Theologico-Politicus" has not yet come to your hands, I will, unless you have any objection, send you a copy. Farewell.

LETTER LIII.
FABRITIUS TO SPINOZA.

[Fabritius, under the order and in the name of the .Elector Palatine, offers Spinoza the post of Professor of Philosophy at Heidelberg, under very liberal conditions.]

Most renowned Sir,—His Most Serene Highness the Elector Palatine, 1 my most gracious master, commands me to write to you, who are, as yet, unknown to me, but most favourably regarded by his Most Serene Highness, and to inquire of you, whether you are willing to accept an ordinary professorship of Philosophy in his illustrious university. An annual salary would be paid to you, equal to that enjoyed at present by the ordinary professors. You will hardly find elsewhere a prince more favourable to distinguished talents, among which he reckons yourself. You will have the most ample freedom in philosophical teaching, which the prince is confident you will not misuse, to disturb the religion publicly established. I cannot refrain from seconding the prince's injunction. I therefore most earnestly beg you to reply as soon as possible, and to address your answer either under cover to the Most Serene Elector's resident at the Hague, Mr. Grotius, or to Mr. Gilles Van der Hele, so that it may come in the packet of letters usually sent to the court, or else to avail yourself of some other convenient opportunity for transmitting it. I will only add, that if you come here, you will live pleasantly a life worthy of a philosopher, unless events turn out quite contrary to our expectation and hope. So farewell.

I remain, illustrious Sir,
Your devoted admirer,
I. LEWIS FABRITIUS.

Professor of the Academy of Heidelberg, and Councillor of the Elector Palatine.

Heidelberg, 16 Feb., 1673.

LETTER LIV.
SPINOZA TO FABRITIUS.

[Spinoza thanks the Elector for his kind offer, but, owing to his unwillingness to teach in public, and other causes, humbly begs to be allowed time to consider it.]

Distinguished Sir,—If I had ever desired to take a professorship in any faculty, I could not have wished for any other than that which is offered to me, through you, by His Most Serene Highness the Elector Palatine, especially because of that freedom in philosophical teaching, which the most gracious prince is kind enough to grant, not to speak of the desire which I have long entertained, to live under the rule of a prince, whom all men admire for his wisdom.

But since it has never been my wish to teach in public, I have been unable to induce myself to accept this splendid opportunity, though I have long deliberated about it. I think, in the first place, that I should abandon philosophical research if I consented to find time for teaching young students. I think, in the second place, that I do not know the limits, within which the freedom of my philosophical teaching would be confined, if I am to avoid all appearance of disturbing the publicly established religion. Religious quarrels do not arise so much from ardent zeal for religion, as from men's various dispositions and love of contradiction, which causes them to habitually distort and condemn everything, however rightly it may have been said. I have experienced these results in my private and secluded station, how much more should I have to fear them after my elevation to this post of honour.

Thus you see, distinguished Sir, that I am not holding back in the hope of getting something better, but through my love of quietness, which I think I can in some measure secure, if I keep away from lecturing in public. I therefore most earnestly entreat you to beg of the Most Serene Elector, that I may be allowed to consider further about this matter, and I also ask you to conciliate the favour of the most gracious prince to his most devoted admirer, thus increasing the obligations of your sincere friend,

B. de. S.

The Hague, 30 March, 1673.

LETTER LV.
HUGO BOXEL TO SPINOZA.

[A friend asks Spinoza's opinion about Ghosts.]

Distinguished Sir,—My reason for writing to you is, that I want to know your opinion about apparitions and ghosts or spectres; if you admit their existence, what do you think about them, and how long does their life last? For some hold them to be mortal, others immortal. As I am doubtful whether you admit their existence, I will proceed no further.

Meanwhile, it is certain, that the ancients believed in them. The theologians and philosophers of to-day are hitherto agreed as to the existence of some creatures of the kind, though they may not agree as to the nature of their essence. Some assert that they are composed of very thin and subtle matter, others that they are spiritual. But, as I was saying before, we are quite at cross purposes, inasmuch as I am doubtful whether you would grant their existence; though, as you must be aware, so many instances and stories of then are found throughout antiquity, that it would really be difficult either to deny or to doubt them. It is clear that, even if you confess that they exist, you do not believe that some of them are the souls of the dead, as the defenders of the Romish faith would have it. I will here end, and will say nothing about war and rumours, inasmuch as our lot is cast in an age, &c. Farewell.

14 Sept., 1674.

LETTER LVI.
SPINOZA TO HUGO BOXEL.

[Spinoza answers that he does not know what ghosts are, and can gain no information from antiquity. (The Hague, Sept., 1674.)]

Dear Sir,—Your letter, which I received yesterday, was most welcome to me, both because I wanted to hear news of you, and also because it shows that you have not utterly forgotten me. Although some might think it a bad omen, that ghosts are the cause of your writing to me, I, on the contrary, can discern a deeper meaning in the circumstance; I see that not only truths, but also things trifling and imaginary may be of use to me.

However, let us defer the question, whether ghosts are delusions and imaginary, for I see that not only denial of them, but even doubt about them seems very singular to you, as to one who has been convinced by the numerous histories related by men of to-day and the ancients. The great esteem and honour, in which I have always held and still hold you, does not suffer me to contradict you, still less to humour you. The middle course, which I shall adopt, is to beg you to be kind enough to select from the numerous stories which you have read, one or two of those least open to doubt, and most clearly demonstrating the existence of ghosts. For, to confess the truth, I have never read a trustworthy author, who clearly showed that there are such things. Up to the present time I do not know what they are, and no one has ever been able to tell me. Yet it is evident, that in the case of a thing so clearly shown by experience we ought to know what it is; otherwise we shall have great difficulty in gathering from histories that ghosts exist. We only gather that something exists of nature unknown. If philosophers choose to call things which we do not know "ghosts," I shall not deny the existence of such, for there are an infinity of things, which I cannot make out.

Pray tell me, my dear Sir, before I explain myself further in the matter, What are these ghosts or spectres? Are they children, or fools, or madmen? For all that I have heard of them seems more adapted to the silly than the wise, or, to say the best we can of it, resembles the pastimes of children or of fools. Before I end, I would submit to you one consideration, namely, that the desire which most men have to narrate things, not as they really happened, but as they wished them to happen, can be illustrated from the stories of ghosts and spectres more easily than from any others. The principal reason for this is, I believe, that such stories are only attested by the narrators, and thus a fabricator can add or suppress circumstances, as seems most convenient to him, without fear of anyone being able to contradict him. He composes them to suit special circumstances, in order to justify the fear he feels of dreams and phantoms, or else to confirm his courage, his credit, or his opinion. There are other reasons, which lead me to doubt, if not the actual stories, at least some of the narrated circumstances; and which have a close bearing on the conclusion we are endeavouring to derive from the aforesaid stories. I will here stop, until I have learnt from you what those stories are, which have so completely convinced you, that you regard all doubt about them as absurd, &c.

LETTER LVII.
HUGO BOXEL TO SPINOZA.

Most sagacious Sir,—You have sent me just the answer I expected to receive, from a friend holding an opinion adverse to my own. But no matter. Friends may always disagree on indifferent subjects without injury to their friendship.

You ask me, before you gave an opinion as to what these spectres or spirits are, to tell you whether they are children, fools, or madmen, and you add that everything you have heard of them seems to have proceeded rather from the insane than the sane. It is a true proverb, which says that a preconceived opinion hinders the pursuit of truth.

I, then, believe that ghosts exist for the following reasons: first, because it appertains to the beauty and perfection of the universe, that they should; secondly, because it is probable that the Creator created them, as being more like Himself than are embodied creatures; thirdly, because as body exists without soul, soul exists without body; fourthly and lastly, because in the upper air, region, or space, I believe there is no obscure body without inhabitants of its own; consequently, that the measureless space between us and the stars is not empty, but thronged with spiritual inhabitants. Perhaps the highest and most remote are true spirits, whereas the lowest in the lowest region of the air are creatures of very thin and subtle substance, and also invisible. Thus I think there are spirits of all sorts, but, perhaps, none of the female sex.

This reasoning will in no wise convince those, who rashly believe that the world has been created by chance. Daily experience, if these reasons be dismissed, shows that there are spectres, and many stories, both new and old, are current about them. Such may be found in Plutarch's book "De viris illustribus," and in his other works; in Suetonius's "Lives of the Cæsars," also in Wierus's and Lavater's books about ghosts, where the subject is fully treated and illustrated from writers of all kinds. Cardano, celebrated for his learning, also speaks of them in his books "De Subtilitate," "De Varietate," and in his "Life;" showing, by experience, that they have appeared to himself, his relations and friends. Melancthon, a wise man and a lover of truth, testifies to his experience of them, as also do many others. A certain burgomaster, learned and wise, who is still living, once told me that he heard by night the noise of working in his mother's brew-house, going on just as it does while beer is being brewed in the day; this he attested as having occurred frequently. The same sort of thing has happened to me, and will never fade from my memory; hence I am convinced by the above-mentioned experiences and reasons, that there are ghosts.

As for evil spirits, who torture wretched men in this life and the next, and who work spells, I believe the stories of them to be fables. In treatises about spirits you will find a host of details. Besides those I have cited, you may refer to Pliny the younger, bk. vii., the letter to Sura; Suetonius, "Life of Julius Cæsar," ch. xxxii.; Valerius Maximus, I. viii. §§ 7, 8; and Alexander ab Alexandro, "Dies Geniales." I am sure these books are accessible to you. I say nothing of monks and priests, for they relate so many tales of souls and evil spirits, or as I should rather say of spectres, that the reader becomes wearied with their abundance. Thymus, a Jesuit, in the book about the apparition of spirits, also treats of the question. But these last-named discourse on such subjects merely for the sake of gain, and to prove that purgatory is not so bad as is supposed, thus treating the question as a mine, from which they dig up plenteous store of gold and silver. But the same cannot be said of the writers mentioned previously, and other moderns, who merit greater credit from their absence of bias.

As an answer to the passage in your letter, where you speak of fools and madmen, I subjoin this sentence from the learned Lavater, who ends with it his first book on ghosts or spectres. "He who is bold enough to gainsay so many witnesses, both ancient and modern, seems to me unworthy of credit. For as it is a mark of frivolity to lend incontinent credence to everyone who says he has seen a ghost; so, on the other hand, rashly and flatly to contradict so many trustworthy historians, Fathers, and other persons placed in authority would argue a remarkable shamelessness."

21 Sept., 1674

LETTER LVIII.
SPINOZA TO HUGO BOXEL.

[Spinoza treats of the necessary creation of the world—he refutes his friend's arguments and quotations.]

Dear Sir,—I will rely on what you said in your letter of the 21st of last month, that friends may disagree on indifferent questions, without injury to their friendship, and will frankly tell you my opinion on the reasons and stories, whereon you base your conclusion, that there are ghosts of every kind, but perhaps none of the female sex. The reason for my not replying sooner is that the books you quoted are not at hand, in fact I have not found any except Pliny and Suetonius. However, these two have saved me the trouble of consulting any other, for I am persuaded that they all talk in the same strain and hanker after extraordinary tales, which rouse men's astonishment and compel their wonder. I confess that I am not a little amazed, not at the stories, but at those who narrate them. I wonder, that men of talent and judgment should so employ their readiness of speech, and abuse it in endeavouring to convince us of such trifles.

However, let us dismiss the writers, and turn to the question itself. In the first place, we will reason a little about your conclusion. Let us see whether I, who deny that there are spectres or spirits, am on that account less able to understand the authors, who have written on the subject; or whether you, who assert that such beings exist, do not give to the aforesaid writers more credit than they deserve. The distinction you drew, in admitting without hesitation spirits of the male sex, but doubting whether any female spirits exist, seems to me more like a fancy than a genuine doubt. If it were really your opinion, it would resemble the common imagination, that God is masculine, not feminine. I wonder that those, who have seen naked ghosts, have not cast their eyes on those parts of the person, which would remove all doubt; perhaps they were timid, or did not know of this distinction. You would say that this is ridicule, not reasoning: and hence I see, that your reasons appear to you so strong and well founded, that no one can (at least in your judgment) contradict them, unless he be some perverse fellow, who thinks the world has been made by chance. This impels me, before going into your reasons, to set forth briefly my opinion on the question, whether the world was made by chance. But I answer, that as it is clear that chance and necessity are two contraries, so is it also clear, that he, who asserts the world to be a necessary effect of the divine nature, must utterly deny that the world has been made by chance; whereas, he who affirms, that God need not have made the world, confirms, though in different language, the doctrine that it has been made by chance; inasmuch as he maintains that it proceeds from a wish, which might never have been formed. However, as this opinion and theory is on the face of it absurd, it is commonly very unanimously admitted, that God's will is eternal, and has never been indifferent; hence it must necessarily be also admitted, you will observe, that the world is a necessary effect of the divine nature. Let them call it will, understanding, or any name they like, they come at last to the same conclusion, that undei different names they are expressing one and the same thing. If you ask them, whether the divine will does not differ from the human, they answer, that the former has nothing in common with the latter except its name; especially as they generally admit that God's will, understanding, intellect, essence, and nature are all identical; so I, myself, lest I should confound the divine nature with the human, do not assign to God human attributes, such as will, understanding, attention, hearing, &c. I therefore say, as I have said already, that the world is a necessary effect of the divine nature, and that it has not been made by chance. I think this is enough to persuade you, that the opinion of those (if such there be), who say that the world has been made by chance, is entirely contrary to mine; and, relying on this hypothesis, I proceed to examine those reasons which lead you to infer the existence of all kinds of ghosts. I should like to say of these reasons generally, that they seem rather conjectures than reasons, and I can with difficulty believe, that you take them for guiding reasons. However, be they conjectures or be they reasons, let us see whether we can take them for foundations.

Your first reason is, that the existence of ghosts is needful for the beauty and perfection of the universe. Beauty, my dear Sir, is not so much a quality of the object beheld, as an effect in him who beholds it. If our sight were longer or shorter, or if our constitution were different, what now appears beautiful to us would seem misshapen, and what we now think misshapen we should regard as beautiful. The most beautiful hand seen through the microscope will appear horrible. Some things are beautiful at a distance, but ugly near; thus things regarded in themselves, and in relation to God, are neither ugly nor beautiful. Therefore, he who says that God has created the world, so that it might be beautiful, is bound to adopt one of the two alternatives, either that God created the world for the sake of men's pleasure and eyesight, or else that He created men's pleasure and eyesight for the sake of the world. Now, whether we adopt the former or the latter of these views, how God could have furthered His object by the creation of ghosts, I cannot see. Perfection and imperfection are names, which do not differ much from the names beauty and ugliness. I only ask, therefore (not to be tedious), which would contribute most to the perfect adornment of the world, ghosts, or a quantity of monsters, such as centaurs, hydras, harpies, satyrs, gryphons, arguses, and other similar inventions? Truly the world would be handsomely bedecked, if God had adorned and embellished it, in obedience to our fancy, with beings, which anyone may readily imagine and dream of, but no one can understand.

Your second reason is, that because spirits express God's image more than embodied creatures, it is probable that He has created them. I frankly confess, that I am as yet in ignorance, how spirits more than other creatures express God. This I know, that between finite and infinite there is no comparison; so that the difference between God and the greatest and most excellent created thing is no less than the difference between God and the least created thing. This argument, therefore, is beside the mark. If I had as clear an idea of ghosts, as I have of a triangle or a circle, I should not in the least hesitate to affirm that they had been created by God; but as the idea I possess of them is just like the ideas, which my imagination forms of harpies, gryphons, hydras, &c., I cannot consider them as anything but dreams, which differ from God as totally, as that which is not differs from that which is.

Your third reason (that as body exists without soul, so soul should exist without body) seems to me equally absurd. Pray tell me, if it is not also likely, that memory, hearing, sight, &c., exist without bodies, because bodies exist without memory, hearing, sight, &c., or that a sphere exists without a circle, because a circle exists without a sphere?

Your fourth, and last reason, is the same as your first, and I refer you to my answer given above. I will only observe here, that I do not know which are the highest or which the lowest places, which you conceive as existing in infinite matter, unless you take the earth as the centre of the universe. For if the sun or Saturn be the centre of the universe, the sun, or Saturn, not the earth, will be the lowest.

Thus, passing by this argument and what remains, I conclude, that these and similar reasons will convince no one of the existence of all kinds of ghosts and spectres, unless it be those persons, who shut their ears to the understanding, and allow themselves to be led away by superstition. This last is so hostile to right reason, that she lends willing credence to old wives' tales for the sake of discrediting philosophers.

As regards the stories, I have already said in my first letter, that I do not deny them altogether, but only the conclusion drawn from them. To this I may add, that I do not believe them so thoroughly, as not to doubt many of the details, which are generally added rather for ornament than for bringing out the truth of the story or the conclusion drawn from it. I had hoped, that out of so many stories you would at least have produced one or two, which could hardly be questioned, and which would clearly show that ghosts or spectres exist. The case you relate of the burgomaster, who wanted to infer their existence, because he heard spectral brewers working in his mother's brewhouse by night, and making the same noises as he was accustomed to hear by day, seems to me laughable. In like manner it would be tedious here to examine all the stories of people, who have written on these trifles. To be brief, I cite the instance of Julius Caesar, who, as Suetonius testifies, laughed at such things and yet was happy, if we may trust what Suetonius says in the 59th chapter of his life of that leader. And so should all, who reflect on the human imagination, and the effects of the emotions, laugh at such notions; whatever Lavater and others, who have gone dreaming with him in the matter, may produce to the contrary.

LETTER LIX.
HUGO BOXEL TO SPINOZA.

[A continuation of the arguments in favour of ghosts, which may be summarized as follows:—I say a thing is done by chance, when it has not been the subject of will on the part of the doer; not when it might never have happened.—Necessity and freedom, not necessity and chance, are contraries.—If we do not in some sense attribute human qualities to God, what meaning can we attach to the term?—You ask for absolute proof of the existence of spirits; such proof is not obtainable for many things, which are yet firmly believed.—Some things are more beautiful intrinsically than others.—As God is a spirit, spirits resemble Him more than embodied creatures do.—A ghost cannot be conceived as clearly as a triangle: can you say that your own idea of God is as clear as your idea of a triangle?—As a circle exists without a sphere, so a sphere exists without a circle.—We call things higher or lower in proportion to their distance from the earth.—All the Stoics, Pythagoreans, and Platonists, Empedocles, Maximus Tyrius, Apuleius, and others, bear witness to ghosts; and no modern denies them. It is presumption to sneer at such a body of testimony. Cæsar did not ridicule ghosts, but omens, and if he had listened to Spurina he would not have been murdered.]

LETTER LX. ,
SPINOZA TO HUGO BOXEL.

[Spinoza again answers the argument in favour of ghosts. (The Hague, 1674).]

Dear Sir,—I hasten to answer your letter, received yesterday, for if I delay my reply, I may have to put it off longer than I should like. The state of your health would have made me anxious, if I did not understand that you are better. I hope you are by this time quite well again.

The difficulties experienced by two people following different principles, and trying to agree on a matter, which depends on many other questions, might be shown from this discussion alone, if there were no reason to prove it by. Pray tell me, whether you have seen or read any philosophers, who hold that the world has been made by chance, taking chance in your sense, namely, that God had some design in making the world, and yet has not kept to the plan he had formed. I do not know, that such an idea has ever entered anyone's mind. I am likewise at a loss for the reasons, with which you want to make me believe, that chance and necessity are not contraries. As soon as I affirm that the three angles of a triangle are equal to two right angles necessarily, I deny that they are thus equal by chance. As soon as I affirm that heat is a necessary effect of fire, I deny that it is a chance effect. To say, that necessary and free are two contrary terms, seems to me no less absurd and repugnant to reason. For no one can deny, that God freely knows Himself and all else, yet all with one voice grant that God knows Himself necessarily. Hence, as it seems to me, you draw no distinction between constraint or force and necessity. Man's wishes to live, to love, &c., are not under constraint, but nevertheless are necessary; much more is it necessary, that God wishes to be, to know, and to act. If you will also reflect, that indifference is only another name for ignorance or doubt, and that a will always constant and determined in all things is a necessary property of the understanding, you will see that my words are in complete harmony with truth. If we affirm, that God might have been able not to wish a given event, or not to understand it, we attribute to God two different freedoms, one necessary, the other indifferent; consequently we shall conceive God's will as different from His essence and understanding, and shall thus fall from one absurdity into another.

The attention, which I asked for in my former letter, has not seemed to you necessary. This has been the reason why you have not directed your thoughts to the main issue, and have neglected a point which is very important.

Further, when you say that if I deny, that the operations of seeing, hearing, attending, wishing, &c., can be ascribed to God, or that they exist in Him in any eminent fashion, you do not know what sort of God mine is; I suspect that you believe there is no greater perfection than such as can be explained by the aforesaid attributes. I am not astonished; for I believe that, if a triangle could speak, it would say, in like manner, that God is eminently triangular, while a circle would say that the divine nature is eminently circular. Thus each would ascribe to God its own attributes, would assume itself to be like God, and look on everything else as ill-shaped.

The briefness of a letter and want of time do not allow me to enter into my opinion on the divine nature, or the questions you have propounded. Besides, suggesting difficulties is not the same as producing reasons. That we do many things in the world from conjecture is true, but that our reflections are based on conjecture is false. In practical life we are compelled to follow what is most probable; in speculative thought we are compelled to follow truth. A man would perish of hunger and thirst, if he refused to eat or drink, till he had obtained positive proof that food and drink would be good for him. But in philosophic reflection this is not so. On the contrary, we must take care not to admit as true anything, which is only probable. For when one falsity has been let in, infinite others follow.

Again, we cannot infer that because sciences of things divine and human are full of controversies and quarrels, therefore their whole subject-matter is uncertain; for there have been many persons so enamoured of contradiction, as to turn into ridicule geometrical axioms. Sextus Empiricus and other sceptics, whom you quote, declare, that it is false to say that a whole is greater than its part, and pass similar judgments on other axioms.

However, as I pass over and grant that in default of proof we must be content with probabilities, I say that a probable proof ought to be such that, though we may doubt about it, we cannot maintain its contrary; for that which can be contradicted resembles not truth but falsehood. For instance, if I say that Peter is alive, because I saw him yesterday in good health, this is a probability, in so far as no one can maintain the contrary; but if anyone says that lie saw Peter yesterday in a swoon, and that he believed Peter to have departed this life to-day, he will make my statement seem false. That your conjecture about ghosts and spectres seems false, and not even probable, I have shown so clearly, that I can find nothing worthy of answer in your reply.

To your question, whether I have of God as clear an idea as I have of a triangle, I reply in the affirmative. But if you ask me, whether I have as clear a mental image of God as I have of a triangle, I reply in the negative. For we are not able to imagine God, though we can understand Him. You must also here observe, that I do not assert that I thoroughly know God, but that I understand some of His attributes, not all nor the greater part, and it is evident that my ignorance of very many does not hinder the knowledge I have of some. When I learned Euclid's Elements, I understood that the three angles of a triangle are equal to two right angles, and this property of a triangle I perceived clearly, though I might be ignorant of many others.

As regards spectres or ghosts, I have hitherto heard attributed to them no intelligible property: they seem like phantoms, which no one can understand. When you say

p. 388

that spectres, or ghosts, in these lower regions (I adopt your phraseology, though I know not why matter below should be inferior to matter above) consist in a very thin rarefied and subtle substance, you seem to me to be speaking of spiders' webs, air, or vapours. To say, that they are. invisible, seems to me to be equivalent to saying that they do not exist, not to stating their nature; unless, perhaps, you wish to indicate, that they render themselves visible or invisible at will, and that the imagination, in these as in other impossibilities, will find a difficulty.

The authority of Plato, Aristotle, and Socrates, does not carry much weight with me. I should have been astonished, if you had brought forward Epicurus, Democritus, Lucretius, or any of the atomists, or upholders of the atomic theory. It is no wonder that persons, who have invented occult qualities, intentional species, substantial forms, and a thousand other trifles, should have also devised spectres and ghosts, and given credence to old wives' tales, in order to take away the reputation of Democritus, whom they were so jealous of, that they burnt all the books which he-had published amid so much eulogy. If you are inclined to believe such witnesses, what reason have you for denying the miracles of the Blessed Virgin, and all the Saints? These have been described by so many famous philosophers, theologians, and historians, that I could produce at least a hundred such authorities for every one of the former. But

I have gone further, my dear Sir, than I intended: I do not desire to cause any further annoyance by doctrines which I know you will not grant. For the principles which you follow are far different from my own.

LETTER LXI.
HUGO BOXEL TO SPINOZA. 1

[Philosophers often differ through using words in different senses. Thus in the question of free will Descartes means by free, constrained t y no cause. You mean by the same, undetermined in a particular way by a cause. The question of free will is threefold:—I. Have we any power whatever over things external to us? II. Have we absolute power over the intentional movements of our own body? III. Have we free use of our reason? Both Descartes and yourself are right according to the terms employed by each (8th October, 1674).]

LETTER LXII.
SPINOZA TO ANON 2 (The Hague, October, 1674).

[Spinoza gives his opinions on liberty and necessity.]

Sir,—Our friend, J. R. 3 has sent me the letter which you have been kind enough to write to me, and also the judgment of your friend 4 as to the opinions of Descartes and myself regarding free will. Both enclosures were very welcome to me. Though I am, at present, much occupied with other matters, not to mention my delicate health, your singular courtesy, or, to name the chief motive, your love of truth, impels me to satisfy your inquiries, as far as my poor abilities will permit. What your friend wishes to imply by his remark before he appeals to experience, I know not. What he adds, that when one of two disputants affirms something which the other denies, both may be right, is true, if he means that the two, though using the same terms, are thinking of different things. I once sent several examples of this to our friend J. R., 1 and am now writing to tell him to communicate them to you.

I, therefore, pass on to that definition of liberty, which he says is my own; but I know not whence he has taken it. I say that a thing is free, which exists and acts solely by the necessity of its own nature. Thus also God understands Himself and all things freely, because it follows solely from the necessity of His nature, that He should understand all things. You see I do not place freedom in free decision, but in free necessity. However, let us descend to created things, which are all determined by external causes to exist and operate in a given determinate manner. In order that this may be clearly understood, let us conceive a very simple thing. For instance, a stone receives from the impulsion of an external cause, a certain quantity of motion, by virtue of which it continues to move after the impulsion given by the external cause has ceased. The permanence of the stone's motion is constrained, not necessary, because it must be defined by the impulsion of an external cause. What is true of the stone is true of any individual, however complicated its nature, or varied its functions, inasmuch as every individual thing is necessarily determined by some external cause to exist and operate in a fixed and determinate manner.

Further conceive, I beg, that a stone, while continuing in motion, should be capable of thinking and knowing, that it is endeavouring, as far as it can, to continue to move. Such a stone, being conscious merely of its own endeavour and not at all indifferent, would believe itself to be completely free, and would think that it continued in motion solely because of its own wish. This is that human freedom, which all boast that they possess, and which consists solely in the fact, that men are conscious of their own desire, but are ignorant of the causes whereby that desire has been determined. Thus an infant believes that it desires milk freely; an angry child thinks he wishes freely for vengeance, a timid child thinks he wishes freely to run away. Again, a drunken man thinks, that from the free decision of his mind he speaks words, which afterwards, when sober, he would like to have left unsaid. So the delirious, the garrulous, and others of the same sort think that they act from the free decision of their mind, not that they are carried away by impulse. As this misconception is innate in all men, it is not easily conquered. For, although experience abundantly shows, that men can do anything rather than check their desires, and that very often, when a prey to conflicting emotions, they see the better course and follow the worse, they yet believe themselves to be free; because in some cases their desire for a thing is slight, and can easily be overruled by the recollection of something else, which is frequently present in the mind.

I have thus, if I mistake not, sufficiently explained my opinion regarding free and constrained necessity, and also regarding so-called human freedom: from what I have said you will easily be able to reply to your friend's objections. For when he says, with Descartes, that he who is constrained by no external cause is free, if by being constrained he means acting against one's will, I grant that we are in some cases quite unrestrained, and in this respect possess free will. But if by constrained he means acting necessarily, although not against one's will (as I have explained above), I deny that we are in any instance free.

But your friend, on the contrary, asserts that we may employ our reason absolutely, that is, in complete freedom; and is, I think, a little too confident on the point. For who, he says, could deny, without contradicting his own consciousness, that I can think with my thoughts, that I wish or do not wish to write? I should like to know what consciousness he is talking of, over and above that which I have illustrated by the example of the stone.

As a matter of fact I, without, I hope, contradicting my consciousness, that is my reason and experience, and without cherishing ignorance and misconception, deny that I can by any absolute power of thought think, that I wish or do not wish to write. I appeal to the consciousness, which he has doubtless experienced, that in dreams he has not the power of thinking that he wishes, or does not wish to write; and that, when he dreams that he wishes to write, he has not the power not to dream that he wishes to write. I think he must also have experienced, that the mind is not always equally capable of thinking of the same object, but according as the body is more capable for the image of this or that object being excited in it, so is the mind more capable of thinking of the same object.

When he further adds, that the causes for his applying his mind to writing have led him, but not constrained him to write, he merely means (if he will look at the question impartially), that his disposition was then in a state, in which it could be easily acted on by causes, which would have been powerless under other circumstances, as for instance when he was under a violent emotion. That is, causes, which at other times would not have constrained him, have constrained him in this case, not to write against his will but necessarily to wish to write.

As for his statement, that if we were constrained by external causes, no one could acquire the habit of virtue, I know not what is his authority for saying, that firmness and constancy of disposition cannot arise from predestined necessity, but only from free will.

What he finally adds, that if this were granted, all wickedness would be excusable, I meet with the question, What then? Wicked men are not less to be feared, and are not less harmful, when they are wicked from necessity. However, on this point I would ask you to refer to my Principles of Cartesian Philosophy, Part II., chap. viii.

In a word, I should like your friend, who makes these objections, to tell me, how he reconciles the human virtue, which he says arises from the free decision of the mind, with God's pre-ordainment of the universe. If, with Descartes, he confesses his inability to do so, he is endeavouring to direct against me the weapon which has already pierced himself. But in vain. For if you examine my opinion attentively, you will see that it is quite consistent, &c.

LETTER LXIII.
FROM ANON. TO SPINOZA. 1

[The writer exhorts Spinoza to publish the treatises on Ethics and on the Improvement of the Understanding.—Remarks on the definition of motion. On the difference between a true and an adequate idea.]

Most excellent Sir,—When shall we have your method of rightly directing the reason in the acquisition of unknown truths, and your general treatise on physics? I know you have already proceeded far with them. The first has already come to my knowledge, and the second I have become aware of from the Lemmas added to the second part of the Ethics; whereby many difficulties in physics are readily solved. If time and opportunity permit, I humbly beg from you a true definition of motion and its explanation; also to know how, seeing that extension in so far as it is conceived in itself is indivisible, immutable, &c., we can infer à priori, that there can arise so many varieties of it, and consequently the existence of figure in the particles of any given body, which are, nevertheless, in every body various, and distinct from the figures of the parts, which compose the reality of any other body. You have already, by word of mouth, pointed out to me a method, which you employ in the search for truths as yet unknown. I find this method to be very excellent, and at the same time very easy, in so far as I have formed an opinion on it, and I can assert that from this single discovery I have made great progress in mathematics. I wish therefore, that you would give me a true definition of an adequate, a true, a false, a fictitious, and a doubtful idea. I have been in search of the difference between a true and an adequate idea. Hitherto, however, I can ascertain nothing except after inquiring into a thing, and forming a certain concept or idea of it. I then (in order to elicit whether this true idea is also an adequate idea of its object) inquire, what is the cause of this idea or concept; when this is ascertained, I again ask, What is the cause of this prior concept? and so I go on always inquiring for the causes of the causes of ideas, until I find a cause of such a kind, that I can not find any cause for it, except that among all the ideas which I can command this alone exists. If, for instance, we inquire the true origin of our errors, Descartes will answer, that it consists in our giving assent to things not yet clearly perceived. But supposing this to be the true idea of the thing, I nevertheless shall not yet be able to determine all things necessary to be known concerning it, unless I have also an adequate idea of the thing in question; in order to obtain such, therefore, I inquire into the cause of this concept, how it happens that we give assent to things not clearly understood—and I answer, that it arises from defective knowledge. But here I cannot inquire further, and ask what is the cause, that we are ignorant of certain things; hence I see that I have detected an adequate idea of the origin of our errors. Here meanwhile I ask you, whether, seeing that many things expressed in infinite modes have an adequate idea of themselves, and that from every adequate idea all that can be known of its object can be inferred, though more readily from some ideas than others, whether, I say, this may be the means of knowing which idea is to be preferred? For instance, one adequate idea of a circle consists in the equality of its radii; another adequate idea consists in the infinite right angles equal to one another, made by the intersection of two lines, &c., and thus we have infinite expressions, each giving the adequate nature of a circle, Now, though all the properties of a circle may be inferred from every one of them, they may be deduced much more easily from some than from others. So also he, who considers lines applied to curves, will be able to draw many conclusions as to the measurement of curves, but will do so more readily from the consideration of tangents, &c. Thus I have wished to indicate how far I have progressed in this study; I await perfection in it, or, if I am wrong on any point, correction; also the definition I asked for. Farewell.

    5 Jan., 1675.

LETTER LXIV.
SPINOZA TO ANON. 1

[The difference between a true and an adequate idea is merely extrinsic, &c. The Hague, Jan., 1675.]

Honoured Sir.—Between a true and an adequate idea, I recognize no difference, except that the epithet true only has regard to the agreement between the idea and its object, whereas the epithet adequate has regard to the nature of the idea in itself; so that in reality there is no difference between a true and an adequate idea beyond this extrinsic relation. However, in order that I may know, from which idea out of many all the properties of its object may be deduced, I pay attention to one point only, namely, that the idea or definition should express the efficient cause of its object. For instance, in inquiring into the properties of a circle, I ask, whether from the idea of a circle, that it consists of infinite right angles, I can deduce all its properties. I ask, I repeat, whether this idea involves the efficient cause of a circle. If it does not, I look for another, namely, that a circle is the space described by a line, of which one point is fixed, and the other movable. As this definition explains the efficient cause, I know that I can deduce from it all the properties of a circle. So, also, when I define God as a supremely perfect Being, then, since that definition does not express the efficient cause (I mean the efficient cause internal as well as external) I shall not be able to infer therefrom all the properties of God; as I can, when I define God as a Being, &c. (see Ethics, I. Def. vi.). As for your other inquiries, namely, that concerning motion, and those pertaining to method, my observations on them are not yet written out in due order, so I will reserve them for another occasion.

As regards your remark, that he "who considers lines applied to curves makes many deductions with regard to the measurement of curves, but does so with greater facility from the consideration of tangents," &c., I think that from the consideration of tangents many deductions will be made with more difficulty, than from the consideration of lines applied in succession; and I assert absolutely, that from certain properties of any particular thing (whatever idea be given) some things may be discovered more readily, others with more difficulty, though all are concerned with the nature of the thing. I think it need only be observed, that an idea should be sought for of such a kind, that all properties may be inferred, as has been said above. He, who is about to deduce all the properties of a particular thing, knows that the ultimate properties will necessarily be the most difficult to discover, &c.

LETTER LXV.
G. H. SCHALLER TO SPINOZA. 1

[Schaller asks for answers to four questions of his friend Tschirnhausen on the attributes of God, and mentions that Tschirnhausen has removed the unfavourable opinion of Spinoza lately conceived by Boyle and Oldenburg.]

Most distinguished and excellent Sir,—I should blush for my silence, which has lasted so long, and has laid me open to the charge of ingratitude for your kindness extended to me beyond my merits, if I did not reflect that your generous courtesy inclines rather to excuse than to accuse, and also know that you devote your leisure, for the common good of your friends, to serious studies, which it would be harmful and injurious to disturb without due cause. For this reason I have been silent, and have meanwhile been content to hear from friends of your good health: I send you this letter to inform you, that our noble friend von Tschirnhausen is enjoying the same in England, and has three times in the letters he has sent me bidden me convey his kindest regards to the master, again bidding me request from you the solution of the following questions, and forward to him your hoped-for answer: would the master be pleased to convince him by positive proof, not by a reduction to the impossible, that we cannot know any attributes of God, save thought and extension? Further, whether it follows that creatures constituted under other attributes can form no idea of extension? If so, it would follow that there must be as many worlds as there are attributes of God. For instance, there would be as much room for extension in worlds affected by other attributes, as there actually exists of extension in our world. But as we perceive nothing save thought besides extension, so creatures in the other world would perceive nothing besides the attributes of that world and thought.

Secondly, as the understanding of God differs from our understanding as much in essence as in existence, it has, therefore, nothing in common with it; therefore (by Ethics, I. iii.) God's understanding cannot be the cause of our own.

Thirdly (in Ethics, I. x. note) you say, that nothing in nature is clearer than that every entity must be conceived under some attribute (this I thoroughly understand), and that the more it has of reality or being, the more attributes appertain to it. It seems to follow from this, that there are entities possessing three, four, or more attributes (though we gather from what has been demonstrated that every being consists only of two attributes, namely, a certain attribute of God and the idea of that attribute).

Fourthly, I should like to have examples of those things which are immediately produced by God, and those which are produced through the means of some infinite modification. Thought and extension seem to be of the former kind; understanding in thought and motion in extension seem to be of the latter.

And these are the points which our said friend von Tschirnhausen joins with me in wishing to have explained by your excellence, if perchance your spare time allows it. He further relates, that Mr. Boyle and Oldenburg had formed a strange idea of your personal character, but that he has not only removed it, but also given reasons, which have not only led them back to a most worthy and favourable opinion thereof, but also made them value most highly the Theologico-Political Treatise. Of this I have not ventured to inform you, because of your health. Be assured that I am, and live,

Most noble sir,
for every good office your most devoted servant,
G. H. SCHALLER.

Amsterdam, 25 July, 1675.

Mr. à Gent and J. Rieuwerts dutifully greet you.

LETTER LXVI.
SPINOZA TO ANON. 1

[Spinoza answers by references to the first three books of the Ethics.]

Dear Sir,—I am glad that you have at last had occasion to refresh me with one of your letters, always most welcome to me. I heartily beg that you will frequently repeat the favour, &c.

I proceed to consider your doubts: to the first I answer, that the human mind can only acquire knowledge of those things which the idea of a body actually existing involves, or of what can be inferred from such an idea. For the power of anything is defined solely by its essence (Ethics, III. vii.); the essence of the mind (Ethics, II. xiii.) consists solely in this, that it is the idea of body actually existing; therefore the mind's power of understanding only extends to things, which this idea of body contains in itself, or which follow therefrom. Now this idea of body does not involve or express any of God's attributes, save extension and thought. For its object (ideatum), namely, body (by Ethics, II. vi), has God for its cause, in so far as He is regarded under the attribute of extension, and not in so far as He is regarded under any other; therefore (Ethics, I. ax. vi.) this idea of the body involves the knowledge of God, only in so far as He is regarded under the attribute of extension. Further, this idea, in so far as it is a mode of thinking, has also (by the same proposition) God for its cause, in so far as He is regarded as a thinking thing, and not in so far as He is regarded under any other attribute. Hence (by the same axiom) the idea of this idea involves the knowledge of God, in so far as He is regarded under the attribute of thought, and not in so far as He is regarded under any attribute. It is therefore plain, that the human mind, or the idea of the human body neither involves nor expresses any attributes of God save these two. Now from these two attributes, or their modifications, no other attribute of God can (Ethics, I. x.) be inferred or conceived. I therefore conclude, that the human mind cannot attain knowledge of any attribute of God besides these, which is the proposition you inquire about. With regard to your question, whether there must be as many worlds as there are attributes, I refer you to Ethics II. vii. note.

Moreover this proposition might be proved more readily by a reduction to the absurd; I am accustomed, when the proposition is negative, to employ this mode of demonstration as more in character. However, as the question you ask is positive, I make use of the positive method, and ask, whether one thing can be produced from another, from which it differs both in essence and existence; for things which differ to this extent seem to have nothing in common. But since all particular things, except those which are produced from things similar to themselves, differ from their causes both in essence and existence, I see here no reason for doubt.

The sense in which I mean that God is the efficient cause of things, no less of their essence than of their existence, I think has been sufficiently explained in Ethics I. xxv. note and corollary. The axiom in the note to Ethics I. x., as I hinted at the end of the said note, is based on the idea which we have of a Being absolutely infinite, not on the fact, that there are or may be beings possessing three, four, or more attributes.

Lastly, the examples you ask for of the first kind are, in thought, absolutely infinite understanding; in extension, motion and rest; an example of the second kind is the sum of the whole extended universe (facies totius universi), which, though it varies in infinite modes, yet remains always the same. Cf. Ethics II. note to Lemma vii. before Prop. xiv.

Thus, most excellent Sir, I have answered, as I think, the objections of yourself and your friend. If you think any uncertainty remains, I hope you will not neglect to tell me, so that I may, if possible, remove it.

The Hague, 29 July, 1675.

LETTER LXVII.
FROM ANON. 1 TO SPINOZA.

[A fresh inquiry as to whether there are two or more attributes of God.]

Distinguished Sir,—I should like a demonstration of what you say: namely, that the soul cannot perceive any attributes of God, except extension and thought. Though this might appear evident to me, it seems possible that the contrary might be deduced from Ethics II. vii. note; perhaps because I do not rightly grasp the meaning of that passage. I have therefore resolved, distinguished Sir, to show you how I make the deduction, earnestly begging you to aid me with your usual courtesy, wherever I do not rightly represent your meaning. I reason as follows:—Though I gather that the universe is one, it is not less clear from the passage referred to, that it is expressed in infinite modes, and therefore that every individual thing is expressed in infinite modes. Hence it seems to follow, that the modification constituting my mind, and the modification constituting my body, though one and the same modification, is yet expressed in infinite ways—first, through thought; secondly, through extension; thirdly, through some attribute of God unknown to me, and so on to infinity, seeing that there are in God infinite attributes, and the order and connection of the modifications seem to be the same in all. Hence arises the question: Why the mind, which represents a certain modification, the same modification being expressed not only in extension, but in infinite other ways,—why, I repeat, does the mind perceive that modification only as expressed through extension, to wit, the human body, and not as expressed through any other attributes? Time does not allow me to pursue the subject further; perhaps my difficulties will be removed by further reflection.

London, 12 Aug., 1675.

LETTER LXVIII.
SPINOZA TO ANON. 1

[In this fragment of a letter Spinoza refers his friend to Ethics, I. x. and II. vii. note.]

Distinguished Sir,—... But in answer to your objection I say, that although each particular thing be expressed in infinite ways in the infinite understanding of God, yet those infinite ideas, whereby it is expressed, cannot constitute one and the same mind of a particular thing, but infinite minds; seeing that each of these infinite ideas has no connection with the rest, as I have explained in the same note to Ethics, II. vii., and as is also evident from I. x. If you will reflect on these passages a little, you will see that all difficulty vanishes, &c.

The Hague, 18 August, 1675.

LETTER LXVIII.A.
G. H. SCHALLER TO SPINOZA.

[Schaller relates to Spinoza Tschirnhausen's doings in France, and letter to him, and makes known to Spinoza the answers contained in that letter to Spinoza's objections in Letter LX VIII. and the request of Leibnitz to see Spinoza's unpublished writings.]

Amsterdam, 14 Nov., 1675.

Most learned and excellent Master, my most venerable Patron,—I hope that you duly received my letter with ——'s method, 1 and likewise, that you are up to the present time in good health, as I am.

But for three months I had no letter from our friend von Tschirnhausen, whence I formed sad conjectures that he had made a fatal journey, when he left England for France. Now that I have received a letter, in my fulness of joy I felt bound, according to his request, to communicate it to the Master, and to let you know, with his most dutiful greeting, that he has arrived safely in Paris, and found there Mr. Huygens, as we had told him, and consequently has in every way sought to please him, and is thus highly esteemed by him. He mentioned, that the Master had recommended to him Huygens's conversation, and made very much of him personally. This greatly pleased Huygens; so he answered that he likewise greatly esteemed you personally, and he has now received from you a copy of the Theologico-Political Treatise, which is esteemed by many there, and it is eagerly inquired, whether there are extant any more of the same writer's works. To this Mr. von Tschirnhausen replied that he knew of none but the Demonstrations in the first and second parts of the Cartesian Principles. But he mentioned nothing about the Master, but what I have said, and so he hopes that he has not displeased you herein.

To the objection that you last made he replies, that those few words which I wrote at the Master's dictation, 1 explained to him your meaning more thoroughly, and that he has favourably entertained the said reasonings (for by these two methods 2 they best admit of explanation). But two reasons have obliged him to continue in the opinion implied in his recent objection. Of these the first is, that otherwise there appears to be a contradiction between the fifth and seventh propositions of the second book. For in the former of these it is laid down, that the objects of ideas are the efficient causes of the ideas, which vet seems to be refuted by the quotation, in the proof of the latter, of the fourth axiom of Part I. "Or, as I rather think, I do not make the right application of this axiom according to the author's intention, which I would most willingly be told by him, if his leisure permits it. The second cause which prevented me from following the explanation he gives was, that thereby the attribute of thought is pronounced to extend much more widely than other attributes. But since every one of the attributes contributes to make up the essence of God, I do not quite see how this fact does not contradict the opinion just stated. I will say just this more, that if I may judge the minds of others by my own, there will be great difficulty in understanding the seventh and eighth propositions of Book II., and this for no other reason than that the author has been pleased (doubtless because they seemed so plain to him) to accompany the demonstrations annexed to them with such short and laconic explanations."

He further mentions, that he has found at Paris a man called Leibnitz, remarkably learned, and most skilled in various sciences, as also free from the vulgar prejudices of theology. With him he has formed an intimate acquaintance, founded on the fact that Leibnitz labours with him to pursue the perfection of the intellect, and, in fact, reckons nothing better or more useful. Von Tschirnhausen says, that he is most practised in ethics, and speaks without any stimulus of the passions by the sole dictate of reason. He adds, that he is most skilled in physics, and also in metaphysical studies concerning God and the soul. Finally, he concludes that he is most worthy of having communicated to him the Master's writings, if you will first give your permission, for he believes that the author will thence gain a great advantage, as he promises to show at length, if the Master be so pleased. But if not, do not doubt, in the least, that he will honourably keep them concealed as he has promised, as in fact he has not made the slightest mention of them. Leibnitz also highly values the Theologico-Political Treatise, on the subject of which he once wrote the Master a letter, if he is not mistaken. And therefore I would beg my Master, that, unless there is some reason against him, you will not refuse your permission in accordance with your gracious kindness, but will, if possible, open your mind to me, as soon as may be, for after receiving your answers I shall be able to reply to our friend von Tschirnhausen, which I would gladly do on Tuesday evening, unless important hindrances cause my Master to delay.

Mr. Bresser, 1 on his return from Cleves, has sent here a large quantity of the beer of that country; I suggested to him that he should make a present to the Master of half a tun, which he promised to do, and added a most friendly greeting.

Finally, excuse my unpractised style and hurried writing, and give me your orders, that I may have a real occasion of proving myself, most excellent Sir,

Your most ready servant,

G. H. SCHALLER.

LETTER LXVIII.B.
SPINOZA TO SCHALLER.

[Spinoza answers all the points in Schaller's letter, and hesitates to entrust his writings to Leibnitz.]

Most experienced Sir, and valued Friend,—I was much pleased to learn from your letter, received to-day, that you are well, and that our friend von Tschirnhausen has happily accomplished his journey to France. In the conversation which he had about me with Mr. Huygens, he behaved, at least in my opinion, very judiciously; and besides, I am very glad that he has found so convenient an opportunity for the purpose which he intended. But what it is he has found in the fourth axiom of Part I. that seems to contradict Proposition v. of Part II. I do not see. For in that proposition it is affirmed, that the essence of every idea has for its cause God, in so far as He is considered as a thinking thing; but in that axiom, that the knowledge or idea of a cause depends on the knowledge or idea of an effect. But, to tell the truth, I do not quite follow, in this matter, the meaning of your letter, and suspect that either in it, or in his copy of the book, there is a slip of the pen. For you write, that it is affirmed in Proposition v. that the objects of ideas are the efficient causes of the ideas, whereas this is exactly what is expressly denied in that proposition, and mow think that this is the cause of the whole confusion. 1 Accordingly it would be useless for me at present to try to write at greater length on this subject, but I must wait, till you explain to me his mind more clearly, and till I know whether he has a correct copy. I believe that I have an epistolary acquaintance with the Leibnitz he mentions. But why he, who was a counsellor at Frankfort, has gone to France, I do not know. As far as I could conjecture from his letters, he seemed to me a man of liberal mind, and versed in every science. But yet I think it imprudent so soon to entrust my writings to him. I should like first to know what is his business in France, and the judgment of our friend von Tschirnhausen, when he has been longer in his company, and knows his character more intimately. However, greet that friend of ours in my name, and let him command me what he pleases, if in anything I can be of service to him, and he will find me most ready to obey him in everything.

I congratulate my most worthy friend Mr. Bresser on his arrival or return, and also thank him heartily for the promised beer, and will requite him, too, in any way that I can. Lastly, I have not yet tried to find out your relation's method, nor do I think that I shall be able to apply my mind to trying it. For the more I think over the thing in itself, the more I am persuaded that you have not made gold, but had not sufficiently eliminated that which was hidden in the antimony. But more of this another time: at present I am prevented by want of leisure. In the meanwhile, if in anything I can assist you, you will always find me, most excellent Sir, your friend and devoted servant,

B. de Spinoza.

The Hague, 18 Nov., 1675.

LETTER LXIX.
FROM ANON. 1 TO SPINOZA.

[The writer asks for explanations of some passages in the letter about the infinite .]

Distinguished Sir,—In the first place I can with great difficulty conceive, how it can be proved, et priori, that bodies exist having motion and figure, seeing that, in extension considered absolutely in itself, nothing of the kind is met with. Secondly, I should like to learn from you, how this passage in your letter on the infinite is to be understood:—"They do not hence infer that such things elude number by the multitude of their component parts." For, as a matter of fact, all mathematicians seem to me always to demonstrate, with regard to such infinities, that the number of the parts is so great, as to elude all expression in terms of number. And in the example you give of the two circles, you do not appear to prove this statement, 2 which was yet what you had undertaken to do. For in this second passage you only show, that they do not draw this conclusion from "the excessive size of the intervening space," or from the fact that "we do not know the maximum and the minimum of the said space;" but you do not demonstrate, as you intended, that the conclusion is not based on the multitude of parts, &e.

2 May, 1676.

LETTER LXX.
SPINOZA TO ANON. 1

[Spinoza explains his view of the infinite.]

Distinguished Sir,—My statement concerning the infinite, that an infinity of parts cannot be inferred from a multitude of parts, is plain when we consider that, if such a conclusion could be drawn from a multitude of parts, we should not be able to imagine a greater multitude of parts; the first-named multitude, whatever it was, would have to be the greater, which is contrary to fact. For in the whole space between two non-concentric circles we conceive a greater multitude of parts than in half that space, yet the number of parts in the half, as in the whole of the space, exceeds any assignable number. Again, from extension, as Descartes conceives it, to wit, a quiescent mass, it is not only difficult, as you say, but absolutely impossible to prove the existence of bodies. For matter at rest, as it is in itself, will continue at rest, and will only be determined to motion by some more powerful external cause; for this reason I have not hesitated on a former occasion to affirm, that the Cartesian principles of natural things are useless, not to say absurd.

The Hague, 5 May, 1676.

LETTER LXXI.
FROM ANON. 1 TO SPINOZA.

[How can the variety of the universe be shown à priori from the Spinozistic conception of extension?]

Most learned Sir,—I wish you would gratify me in this matter by pointing out how, from the conception of extension, as you give it, the variety of the universe can be shown à priori. You recall the opinion of Descartes, wherein he asserts, that this variety can only be deduced from extension, by supposing that, when motion was started by God, it caused this effect in extension. Now it appears to me, that he does not deduce the existence of bodies from matter at rest, unless, perhaps, you count as nothing the assumption of God as a motive power; you have not shown how such an effect must, à priori, necessarily follow from the nature of God. A difficulty which Descartes professed himself unable to solve as being beyond human understanding. I therefore ask you the question, knowing that you have other thoughts on the matter, unless perhaps there be some weighty cause for your unwillingness hitherto to disclose your opinion. If this, as I suppose, be not expedient, give me some hint of your meaning. You may rest assured, that whether you speak openly with me, or whether you employ reserve, my regard for you will remain unchanged.

My special reasons for making the requests are as follows:—I have always observed in mathematics, that from a given thing considered in itself, that is, from the definition of a given thing, we can only deduce a single property; if, however, we require to find several properties, we are obliged to place the thing defined in relation to other things. Then from the conjunction of the definitions of these things new properties result. For instance, if I regard the circumference of a circle by itself, I can only infer that it is everywhere alike or uniform, in which property it differs essentially from all other curves; I shall never be able to infer any other properties. But if I place it in relation with other things, such as the radii drawn from the centre, two intersecting lines, or many others, I shall be able hence to deduce many properties; this seems to be in opposition to Prop. xvi. of your Ethics, almost the principal proposition of the first book of your treatise. For it is there assumed as known, that from the given definition of anything several properties can be deduced. This seems to me impossible, unless we bring the thing defined into relation with other things; and further, I am for this reason unable to see, how from any attribute regarded singly, for instance, infinite extension, a variety of bodies can result; if you think that this conclusion cannot be drawn from one attribute considered by itself, but from all taken together, I should like to be instructed by you on the point, and shown how it should be conceived.—Farewell, &c.

Paris, 23 June, 1676.

LETTER LXXII.
SPINOZA TO

[Spinoza gives the required explanation. Mentions the treatise of Huet, &c.]

Distinguished Sir,—With regard to your question as to whether the variety of the universe can be deduced à priori from the conception of extension only, I believe I have shown clearly enough already that it cannot; and that, therefore, matter has been ill-defined by Descartes as extension; it must necessarily be explained through an attribute, which expresses eternal and infinite essence. But perhaps, some day, if my life be prolonged, I may discuss the subject with you more clearly. For hitherto I have not been able to put any of these matters into due order.

As to what you add; namely, that from the definition of a given thing considered in itself we can only deduce a single property, this is, perhaps, true in the case of very simple things (among which I count figures), but not in realities. For, from the fact alone, that I define God as a Being to whose essence belongs existence, I infer several of His properties; namely, that He necessarily exists, that He is One, unchangeable, infinite, &c. I could adduce several other examples, which, for the present, I pass over.

In conclusion, I ask you to inquire, whether Huet's treatise (against the "Tractatus Theologico-Politicus") about which I wrote to you before, has yet been published, and whether you could send me a copy. Also, whether you yet know, what are the new discoveries about refraction. And so farewell, dear Sir, and continue to regard yours, &c.

The Hague, 15 July, 1676.

LETTER LXXIII.
ALBERT BURGH TO SPINOZA.

[Albert Burgh announces his reception into the Romish Church, and exhorts Spinoza to follow his example. 1]

I promised to write to you on leaving my country, if anything noteworthy occurred on the journey. I take the opportunity which offers of an event of the utmost importance, to redeem my engagement, by informing you that I have, by God's infinite mercy, been received into the Catholic Church and made a member of the same. You may learn the particulars of the step from a letter which I have sent to the distinguished and accomplished Professor Craanen of Leyden. I will here subjoin a few remarks for your special benefit.

Even as formerly I admired you for the subtlety and keenness of your natural gifts, so now do I bewail and deplore you; inasmuch as being by nature most talented, and adorned by God with extraordinary gifts; being a lover, nay a coveter of the truth, you yet allow yourself to be ensnared and deceived by that most wretched and most proud of beings, the prince of evil spirits. As for all your philosophy, what is it but a mere illusion and chimera? Yet to it you entrust not only your peace of mind in this life, but the salvation of your soul for eternity. See on what a wretched foundation all your doctrines rest. You assume that you have at length discovered the true philosophy. How do you know that your philosophy is the best of all that ever have been taught in the world, are now being taught, or ever shall be taught? Passing over what may be devised in the future, have you examined all the philosophies, ancient as well as modern, which are taught here, and in India, and everywhere throughout the whole world? Even if you have duly examined them, how do you know that you have chosen the best? You will say: "My philosophy is in harmony with right reason; other philosophies are not." But all other philosophers except your own followers disagree with you, and with equal right say of their philosophy what you say of yours, accusing you, as you do them, of falsity and error. It is, therefore, plain, that before the truth of your philosophy can come to light, reasons must be advanced, which are not common to other philosophies, but apply solely to your own; or else you must admit that your philosophy is as uncertain and nugatory as the rest.

However, restricting myself for the present to that book of yours with an impious title, 1 and mingling your philosophy with your theology, as in reality you mingle them yourself, though with diabolic cunning you endeavour to maintain, that each is separate from the other, and has different principles, I thus proceed.

Perhaps you will say: "Others have not read Holy Scripture so often as I have; and it is from Holy Scripture, the acknowledgment of which distinguishes Christians from the rest of the world, that I prove my doctrines. But how? By comparing the clear passages with the more obscure I explain Holy Scripture, and out of my interpretations I frame dogmas, or else confirm those which are already concocted in my brain." But, I adjure you, reflect seriously on what you say. How do you know, that you have made a right application of your method, or again that your method is sufficient for the interpretation of Scripture, and that you are thus interpreting Scripture aright, especially as the Catholics say, and most truly, that the universal Word of God is not handed down to us in writing, hence that Holy Scripture cannot be explained through itself, I will not say by one man, but by the Church herself, who is the sole authorized interpreter? The Apostolic traditions must likewise be consulted, as is proved by the testimony of Holy Scripture and. Thus,

Fathers, and as reason and experience suggest. your first principles are most false and lead to destruction, what will become of all your doctrine, built up and supported on so rotten a foundation?

Wherefore, if you believe in Christ crucified, acknowledge your pestilent heresy, reflect on the perverseness of your nature, and be reconciled with the Church.

How do your proofs differ from those of all heretics, who ever have left, are now leaving, or shall in future leave God's Church? All, like yourself, make use of the same principle, to wit, Holy Scripture taken by itself, for the concoction and establishment of their doctrines.

Do not flatter yourself with the thought, that neither the Calvinists, it may be, nor the so-called Reformed Church, nor the Lutherans, nor the Mennonites, nor the Socinians, &c., can refute your doctrines. All these, as I have said, are as wretched as yourself, and like you are dwelling in the shadow of death.

If you do not believe in Christ, you are more wretched than I can express. Yet the remedy is easy. Turn away from your sins, and consider the deadly arrogance of your wretched and insane reasoning. You do not believe in Christ. Why? You will say: "Because the teaching and the life of Christ, and also the Christian teaching concerning Christ are not at all in harmony with my teaching." But again, I say, then you dare to think yourself greater than all those who have ever risen up in the State or Church of God, patriarchs, prophets, apostles, martyrs, doctors, confessors, and holy virgins innumerable, yea, in your blasphemy, than Christ himself. Do you alone surpass all these in doctrine, in manner of life, in every respect? Will you, wretched pigmy, vile worm of the earth, yea, ashes, food of worms, will you in your unspeakable blasphemy, dare to put yourself before the incarnate, infinite wisdom of the Eternal Father? Will you, alone, consider yourself wiser and greater than all those, who from the beginning of the world have been in the Church of God, and have believed, or believe still, that Christ would come or has already come? On what do you base this rash, insane, deplorable, and inexcusable arrogance?

If you cannot pronounce on what I have just been enumerating (divining rods, alchemy, &c.), why, wretched man, are you so puffed up with diabolical pride, as to pass rash judgment on the awful mysteries of Christ's life and passion, which the Catholics themselves in their teaching declare to be incomprehensible? Why do you commit the further insanity of silly and futile carping at the numberless miracles and signs, which have been wrought through the virtue of Almighty God by the apostles and disciples of Christ, and afterwards by so many thousand saints, in testimony to, and confirmation of the truth of the Catholic faith; yea, which are being wrought in our own time in cases without number throughout the world, by God's almighty goodness and mercy? If you cannot gainsay these, and surely you cannot, why stand aloof any longer? Join hands of fellowship, and repent from your sins: put on humility, and be born again.

[Albert Burgh requests Spinoza to consider: (i.) The large number of believers in the Romish faith. (ii.) The uninterrupted succession of the Church. (iii.) The fact that a few unlearned men converted the world to Christianity. (iv.) The antiquity, the immutability, the infallibility, the incorruption, the unity, and the vast extent of the Catholic Religion; also the fact, that secession from it involves damnation, and that it will itself endure as long as the world. (v.) The admirable organization of the Romish Church. (vi.) The superior morality of Catholics. (vii.) The frequent cases of recantation of opinions among heretics. (viii.) The miserable life led by atheists, whatever their outward demeanour may be.]

I have written this letter to you with intentions truly Christian; first, in order to show the love I bear to you, though you are a heathen; secondly, in order to beg you not to persist in converting others.

I therefore will thus conclude: God is willing to snatch your soul from eternal damnation, if you will allow Him. Do not doubt that the Master, who has called you so often through others, is now calling you for the last time through me, who having obtained grace from the ineffable mercy of God Himself, beg the same for you with my whole heart. Do not deny me. For if you do not now give ear to God who calls you, the wrath of the Lord will be kindled against you, and there is a danger of your being abandoned by His infinite mercy, and becoming a wretched victim of the Divine Justice which consumes all things in wrath. Such a fate may Almighty God avert for the greater glory of His name, and for the salvation of your soul, also for a salutary example for the imitation of your most unfortunate and idolatrous followers, through our Lord and Saviour Jesus Christ, Who with the Eternal Father liveth and reigneth in the Unity of the Holy Spirit, God for all Eternity. Amen.

Florence, III. Non. Sept. CICICCLXXV. (Sept. 3, 1675.) 1

LETTER LXXIV. SPINOZA TO ALBERT BURGH.

[Spinoza laments the step taken by his pupil, and answers his arguments. The Hague, end of 1675.]

That, which I could scarcely believe when told me by others, I learn at last from your own letter; not only have you been made a member of the Romish Church, but you are become a very keen champion of the same, and have already learned wantonly to insult and rail against your opponents.

At first I resolved to leave your letter unanswered, thinking that time and experience will assuredly be of more avail than reasoning, to restore you to yourself and your friends; not to mention other arguments, which won your approval formerly, when we were discussing the case of Steno, 1 in whose steps you are now following. But some of my friends, who like myself had formed great hopes from your superior talents, strenuously urge me not to fail in the offices of a friend, but to consider what you lately were, rather than what you are, with other arguments of the like nature. I have thus been induced to write you this short reply, which I earnestly beg you will think worthy of calm perusal.

I will not imitate those adversaries of Romanism, who would set forth the vices of priests and popes with a view to kindling your aversion. Such considerations are often put forward from evil and unworthy motives, and tend rather to irritate than to instruct. I will even admit, that more men of learning and of blameless life are found in the Romish Church than in any other Christian body; for, as it contains more members, so will every type of character be more largely represented in it. You cannot possibly deny, unless you have lost your memory as well as your reason, that in every Church there are thoroughly honourable men, who worship God with justice and charity. We have known many such among the Lutherans, the Reformed Church, the Mennonites, and the Enthusiasts. Not to go further, you knew your own relations, who in the time of the Duke of Alva suffered every kind of torture bravely and willingly for the sake of their religion. In fact, you must admit, that personal holiness is not peculiar to the Romish Church, but common to all Churches.

As it is by this, that we know "that we dwell in God and He in us" (1 Ep. John, iv. 13), it follows, that what distinguishes the Romish Church from others must be something entirely superfluous, and therefore founded solely on superstition. For, as John says, justice and charity are the one sure sign of the true Catholic faith, and the true fruits of the Holy Spirit. Wherever they are found, there in truth is Christ; wherever they are absent, Christ is absent also. For only by the Spirit of Christ can we be led to the love of justice and charity. Had you been willing to reflect on these points, you would not have ruined yourself, nor have brought deep affliction on your relations, who are now sorrowfully bewailing your evil case.

But I return to your letter, which you begin, by lamenting that I allow myself to be ensnared by the prince of evil spirits. Pray take heart, and recollect yourself. When you had the use of your faculties, you were wont, if I mistake not, to worship an Infinite God, by Whose efficacy all things absolutely come to pass and are preserved; now you dream of a prince, God's enemy, who against God's will ensnares and deceives very many men (rarely good ones, to be sure), whom God thereupon hands over to this master of wickedness to be tortured eternally. The Divine justice therefore allows the devil to deceive men and remain unpunished; but it by no means allows to remain unpunished the men, who have been by that self-same devil miserably deceived and ensnared.

These absurdities might so far be tolerated, if you worshipped a God infinite and eternal; not one whom Chastillon, in the town which the Dutch call Tienen, gave with impunity to horses to be eaten. And, poor wretch, you bewail me? My philosophy, which you never beheld, you style a chimera? O youth deprived of understanding, who has bewitched you into believing, that the Supreme and Eternal is eaten by you, and held in your intestines?

Yet you seem to wish to employ reason, and ask me, "How I know that my philosophy is the best among all that have ever been taught in the world, or are being taught, or ever will be taught?" a question which I might with much greater right ask you; for I do not presume that I have found the best philosophy, I know that I understand the true philosophy. If you ask in what way I know it, I answer: In the same way as you know that the three angles of a triangle are equal to two right angles: that this is sufficient, will be denied by no one whose brain is sound, and who does not go dreaming of evil spirits inspiring us with false ideas like the true. For the truth is the index of itself and of what is false.

But you; who presume that you have at last found the best religion, or rather the best men, on whom you have pinned your credulity, you, "who know that they are the best among all who have taught, do now teach, or shall in future teach other religions. Have you examined all religions, ancient as well as modern, taught here and in India and everywhere throughout the world? And, if you have duly examined them, how do you know that you have chosen the best" since you can give no reason for the faith that is in you? But you will say, that you acquiesce in the inward testimony of the Spirit of God, while the rest of mankind are ensnared and deceived by the prince of evil spirits. But all those outside the pale of the Romish Church can with equal right proclaim of their own creed what you proclaim of yours.

As to what you add of the common consent of myriads of men and the uninterrupted ecclesiastical succession, this is the very catch-word of the Pharisees. They with no less confidence than the devotees of Rome bring forward their myriad witnesses, who as pertinaciously as the Roman witnesses repeat what they have heard, as though it were their personal experience. Further, they carry back their line to Adam. They boast with equal arrogance, that their Church has continued to this day unmoved and unimpaired in spite of the hatred of Christians and heathen. They more than any other sect are supported by antiquity. They exclaim with one voice, that they have received their traditions from God Himself, and that they alone preserve the Word of

God both written and unwritten. That all heresies have issued from them, and that they have remained constant through thousands of years under no constraint of temporal dominion, but by the sole efficacy of their superstition, no one can deny. The miracles they tell of would tire a thousand tongues. But their chief boast is, that they count a far greater number of martyrs than any other nation, a number which is daily increased by those who suffer with singular constancy for the faith they profess; nor is their boasting false. I myself knew among others of a certain Judah called the faithful, 1 who in the midst of the flames, when he was already thought to be dead, lifted his voice to sing the hymn beginning, "To Thee, O God, I offer up my soul," and so singing perished.

The organization of the Roman Church, which you so greatly praise, I confess to be politic, and to many lucrative. I should believe that there was no other more convenient for deceiving the people and keeping men's minds in check, if it were not for the organization of the Mahometan Church, which far surpasses it. For from the time when this superstition arose, there has been no schism in its church.

If, therefore, you had rightly judged, you would have seen that only your third point tells in favour of the Christians, namely, that unlearned and common men should have been able to convert nearly the whole world to a belief in Christ. But this reason militates not only for the Romish Church, but for all those who profess the name of Christ.

But assume that all the reasons you bring forward tell in favour solely of the Romish Church. Do you think that you can thereby prove mathematically the authority of that Church? As the case is far otherwise, why do you wish me to believe that my demonstrations are inspired by the prince of evil spirits, while your own are inspired by God, especially as I see, and as your letter clearly shows, that you have been led to become a devotee of this Church not by your love of God, but by your fear of hell, the single cause of superstition? Is this your humility, that you trust nothing to yourself, but everything to others, who are condemned by many of their fellow men? Do you set it down to pride and arrogance, that I employ reason and acquiesce in this true Word of God, which is in the mind and can never be depraved or corrupted? Cast away this deadly superstition, acknowledge the reason which God has given you, and follow that, unless you would be numbered with the brutes. Cease, I say, to call ridiculous errors mysteries, and do not basely confound those things which are unknown to us, or have not yet been discovered, with what is proved to be absurd, like the horrible secrets of this Church of yours, which, in proportion as they are repugnant to right reason, you believe to transcend the understanding.

But the fundamental principle of the "Tractatus Theologico-Politicus," that Scripture should only be expounded through Scripture, which you so wantonly without any reason proclaim to be false, is not merely assumed, but categorically proved to be true or sound; especially in chapter vii., where also the opinions of adversaries are confuted; see also what is proved at the end of chapter xv. If you will reflect on these things, and also examine the history of the Church (of which I see you are completely ignorant), in order to see how false, in many respects, is Papal tradition, and by what course of events and with what cunning the Pope of Rome six hundred years after Christ obtained supremacy over the Church, I do not doubt that you will eventually return to your senses. That this result may come to pass I, for your sake, heartily wish. Farewell, &c.

LETTER LXXV.
SPINOZA TO LAMBERT VAN VELTHUYSEN (Doctor of Medicine at Utrecht.) 1

[Of the proposed annotation of the "Tractatus Theologico-Politicus."]

Most excellent and distinguished Sir,—I wonder at our friend Neustadt having said, that I am meditating the refutation of the various writings circulated against my book, 1 and that among the works for me to refute he places your MS. For I certainly have never entertained the intention of refuting any of my adversaries: they all seem to me utterly unworthy of being answered. I do not remember to have said to Mr. Neustadt anything more, than that I proposed to illustrate some of the obscurer passages in the treatise with notes, and that I should add to these your MS., and my answer, if your consent could be gained, on which last point I begged him to speak to you, adding, that if you refused permission on the ground, that some of the observations in my answer were too harshly put, you should be given full power to modify or expunge them. In the meanwhile, I am by no means angry with Mr. Neustadt, but I wanted to put the matter before you as it stands, that if your permission be not granted, I might show you that I have no wish to publish your MS. against your will. Though I think it might be issued without endangering your reputation, if it appears without your name, I will take no steps in the matter, unless you give me leave. But, to tell the truth, you would do me a far greater kindness, if you would put in writing the arguments with which you think you can impugn my treatise, and add them to your MS. I most earnestly beg you to do this. For there is no one whose arguments I would more willingly consider; knowing, as I do, that you are bound solely by your zeal for truth, and that your mind is singularly candid, I therefore beg you again and again, not to shrink from undertaking this task, and to believe me, Yours most obediently,

b. de Spinoza.

www.ingramcontent.com/pod-product-compliance
Lightning Source LLC
Chambersburg PA
CBHW030525100426
42813CB00001B/159